Service Thinking

Service Thinking

The Seven Principles to Discover Innovative Opportunities

Hunter Hastings and Jeff Saperstein

businessexpert
Press

First published in 2014 by
Business Expert Press, LLC
222 East 46th Street, New York, NY 10017
www.businessexpertpress.com

ISBN-13: 978-1-60649-662-6 (paperback)
ISBN-13: 978-1-60649-663-3 (e-book)

Business Expert Press Service Systems and Innovations in Business and Society Collection

Collection ISSN: 2326-2664 (print)
Collection ISSN: 2326-2699 (electronic)

Cover and interior design by Exeter Premedia Services Private Ltd., Chennai, India

First edition: 2014

10 9 8 7 6 5 4 3 2 1

Printed in the United States of America.

In Memory
Doug Engelbart
1925–2013

Abstract

Business paradigm shifts are rare. However, the shift to a service-dominant economy and to service-dominant value creation genuinely merits such a designation, both on the surface through the lens of traditional economic measures and even more deeply and profoundly through the lens of Vargo and Lusch's Service-Dominant Logic (S-D Logic). Almost 80% of GDP in developed economies is attributable to services, and some economists regard products as merely the physical embodiment of service delivery. Yet today's business analysis, business management, business organization, business processes, and business education emerged from a manufacturing-dominant logic; the principles of service are often underserved and poorly understood. This results in lost opportunities for growth.

Service Science, Management and Engineering (SSME) has been slowly bubbling up and building learning and knowledge in academia for 30 years, with an acceleration in the last 10 years. The disciplines, principles, insights and tools of SSME are now ready to transition to the mainstream business world, with transformative effect.

This book begins with expository case histories of the SSME-based transformation of familiar businesses. It then expounds the seven principles of service science, with compelling examples and clear direction for application. It describes the tools for application of the principles, from modular business architecture (a new form of business organization to achieve absolute advantage) to the Glo-Mo-So (global, mobile, and social) business tools that establish scalable platforms for fast, efficient growth in the service economy for Globally Integrated Enterprises—large and small/medium enterprises (SME).

The first principle—from which all else logically follows—is that value is co-created. "Value co-creation" changes all roles: the role of the customer vis-a-vis the provider, the role of the employee vis-a-vis the hierarchy, the role of the specialist company vis-a-vis the giant corporation. S-D Logic Fundamental Proposition (FP) 10 states that value is uniquely and phenomenologically determined by the beneficiary. FP 7 states that the enterprise cannot deliver value, but only offer value propositions.

Value co-creation is the force behind the rise of social business tools. The "social approach" (to business, to branding, to innovation, etc.) emphasizes winning by "fitting in" and "contributing", and to do so well requires new ways of analyzing trends in society, business, and industry architecture. This is as true for the individual as it is for the enterprise. Service science emphasizes the T-shape, combining both specialized depth (the vertical in the T) and breadth of comprehension and understanding (the horizontal in the T). Both are required for success—for enterprises and individuals.

Social business tools are reflective of service systems, assembled from knowledge, technology, and value propositions to create perfected service outcomes and experiences. Modularized business architectures are the route to optimizing participation in service systems, and Component Business Model (CBM) is one specific tool to design such as architecture.

Social business tools generate "big data," requiring new methods and ways of incorporating analytics, including predictive modeling. Learning is always dynamic in social science, adhering to the principle of Run-Transform-Innovate for continuous improvement.

Service science, as a field of academic study and research, is supported by 30 years of learning. This book brings this knowledge firmly into the business mainstream, addressing both the "Why" and the "How," and incorporating the tools for action.

Keywords

service science, value, co-creation, service system, modularization, analytics, marketing

Contents

Foreword

Leaders in every industry are reshaping their strategies to succeed in this era of relentless change and discontinuity.

Today, the average large company can expect a shorter lifespan than the average human, and competition has become tougher, with profit margins under constant pressure. Smart leaders are seeking radical new ways of thinking to navigate through these uncharted waters and meet the demands of new competition, new customer expectations, and new economics.

The modern global economy—with all its change and uncertainty—is just as challenging for individuals as it is for organizations. How do you navigate a successful, enduring career in such a dynamic environment?

The major lesson we have learned at IBM is that a commitment to ongoing transformation is the only path to enduring success. Both organizations and individuals need to be skilled at managing change and equipped with the flexibility to respond in real time to shifting market conditions. With all its risks, this new era offers enormous opportunity for innovators who can harness the platforms, analytics, and new strategies that this book propounds.

Several years ago, in my book *Let Go To Grow: Escaping the Commodity Trap*, I identified the componentized business model as key to enterprise innovation. The core concept we described is to build a business built on a set of configurable components and a technology platform that provides the ability to respond to the unpredictable and uncontrollable with speed, flexibility and adaptability. We also highlighted some firms that are pioneers in value co-creation, finding unique ways to collaborate with customers, partners and suppliers.

In the book, we emphasized the need for a disciplined approach to letting go of the past to invest more in future growth opportunities—the discipline of run-transform-innovate. This business model—being able to jettison fixed cost burdens so as to be able to move ahead to better customer service—lies at the core of Service Thinking.

The authors of *Service Thinking* have expanded on the idea of co-created value, demonstrating with vivid case studies and clear analysis a framework that is understandable, usable, and compelling. The book offers a wealth of practical ideas for both organizations and individuals seeking to pursue the path of innovation and perpetual reinvention—the only strategy for success in the 21st century global knowledge economy.

Linda S. Sanford

IBM Senior Vice President, Enterprise Transformation

Preface

We realized when we concluded our last book, *Bust the Silos: Opening Your Organization for Growth* (Create Space, 2010), that while we initially targeted the content to mature professional business executives in large organizations, we also had hoped to speak to a new generation of professionals who had a different set of business values than their predecessors.

As the members of the first digital native generation in history take their place in the business world, they bring a mindset that will challenge and change many institutions, countries, and cultures. The following chart summarizes some of the differences in values and aspirations between generations.

Baby boomer values	Millennial values
Company identity	Autonomy
Field of practice	Mastery
Proprietary knowledge	Sharing/collaboration
Department/function	Roles/T-Shaped individuals who can work with multiple disciplines
Compartmentalize	Higher purpose
Work, then life fits in	Life balance
Upward mobility	Curating experiences

Different times and mindsets require different approaches to business and organizational development. Our work in both international marketing as well as teaching in graduate business schools has reinforced our belief that this time and this context are perfect for a popular introduction to Service Thinking. The Millennial generation is demanding and accelerating change, but so are those who choose to innovate to create businesses or reinvigorate existing ones, and are engaging in new business models, requiring new thinking. Some of the factors driving this are:

1. New technologies of Internet-based social engagement for customer and employee utilization are being co-created at the edge of the network and not directed from the C-Suite down.

2. Big data integration for effective data analysis to support more pre-cise identification of growth and revenue opportunities is taking strategy development from the exclusivity of the boardroom to the ubiquity of the lunchroom.

3. Acceleration of the service economy is a global phenomenon. Even Hong Kong—previously known as one of the Asian manufacturing Tigers—now derives over 93% of its GDP from services.[1]

4. The change in organizational design from vertical, "silo" depart-ments and corporations to more permeable shared value networks of project-based teams across organizations is unleashing innovation.

5. There is a yearning of a new generation for an entrepreneurial work environment where autonomy, mastery of competencies (T-shaped individuals), sharing and collaboration with peers, and work focused toward higher values for the common good are encouraged, recog-nized, and rewarded.

And now that the tools and infrastructure are ready, businesses can con-template the compelling reasons for the application of Service Thinking principles:

1. Service is the source of new and energetic growth in economies—at the national, state, city, and enterprise levels. Service is high margin, and fast evolving. Service takes advantage of modern infrastructure innovations in global technologies, mobile communications, and social business platforms. All economies, from developed to emerg-ing, can find advantage in the service approach.

2. Better service is co-created between providers and customers. The benefits customers receive are therefore at a higher level, because cus-tomers help design those benefits. Their needs are met in a more desirable manner. The result is a higher quality of life for individuals and communities. Service Thinking unlocks enhanced quality of life.

3. There is a skills gap in all economies between traditional skills and those required for service delivery, whether in organization architecture (design, management, engineering, measurement, com-munications) or on the front line of service delivery (responsiveness, empathy, empowerment, flexibility, interpersonal communications,

decision-making). Service Thinking can bridge this gap and lead to higher collective intelligence and responsiveness; thereby better employing individuals for productive careers to provide every individual with the path to a more fulfilled purpose in life—being of service to others, to their community, and to the planet.

Who Should Read This Book?

We hope anyone who is seriously considering how to guide an enterprise and his/her career would benefit from this book. However, there are three primary groups we believe will have the most interest.

Entrepreneurs and Start-ups

New businesses have the advantage of fewer legacy constraints that inhibit their growth. However, many entrepreneurs may lack an effective business strategy to take advantage of the opportunities that can be gleaned through a disciplined approach to building a business based on co-creation of value with customers and the other concepts in the Service Thinking framework that could focus the business to rapidly scale and succeed.

Managers in Global Integrated Enterprises (GIEs)

Traditional multinational corporations are under great pressure to adapt rapidly to some of the changes we have identified. Managers across different functional areas such as marketing, sales, finance, customer support, and product/service development are seeking proven, evidence-based ways to improve their opportunities to serve their existing customer base.

Regional Small and Medium Sized Enterprises (RSMEs)

What may have worked in the past to create and sustain a viable business may no longer be adequate to survive new, disruptive entrants who can utilize newer technologies and approaches (such as specialization and integration) to undermine a whole category (systems that provide services to a customer such as in healthcare, transportation, etc.). Service Thinking can provide RSMEs with a way to grow and change without jeopardizing the customer base and product/service portfolio that has sustained the business to date.

By acquainting readers with the principles, tools, and methods of Service Thinking, we hope readers can identify and implement initiatives for increased opportunity for effectiveness, revenue growth, and profit leading to a smarter planet, smarter regions, smarter universities, smarter organizations, and smarter partnerships with customers.

   We also hope this book will contribute to the field of Service Science; that it can help to encourage wider adoption of Service Science as a field of study in Business Universities, and advance Service Thinking as a recognized, valued competency among business enterprises. We would most hope that our efforts would help to democratize the application of Service Thinking for the greater good.

Acknowledgments

There are many people who contributed their support in time, talents, intellectual property, and encouragement to this project, whom we wish to acknowledge.

Foremost are Jim Spohrer and Jorge Sanz from IBM who championed and guided us with their generous support in time, expertise in business modeling for different industries, operational strategy tools, componentized business architecture, and advice. They have dedicated their career focus to Service Science and Component Business Modeling and we are honored that they enabled us to write this book.

We have a special thanks to Haluk Demirkan, who both championed and edited our work, and to Yassi Moghaddam who has helped to enable Service Thinking to be reviewed through ISSIP (International Society for Service Innovation Professionals).

In addition, we want to acknowledge other IBMers who supported us with their insights: Linda Sanford, Daryl Pereira, Sara Moulton Reger, and Wendy Murphy.

We are grateful to those at Hult International Business School, who enabled us to pilot the Service Thinking program in the MBA program. Our thanks to: Steve Hodges, Nick van der Walt, Luis Umana Timms, Larry Louie, Marty Manley, and Marjan Mohsenin.

Special thanks to those whom we profiled that exemplify Service Thinking in their enterprises: Rajat Paharia, Dr. Sam Pejham, Steve Susskind, Ben Chun, and Mike Saperstein.

Thanks to our assistant Barkha Shah and the students at Hult International Business School who have helped us to learn about Service Thinking through teaching them.

Introduction

We are in the early throes of a Great Restructuring. Our technologies are racing ahead but many of our skills and organizations are lagging behind. So it is urgent that we understand these phenomena, discuss their implications, and come up with strategies that allow human workers to race ahead with machines instead of racing against them.[1]

—Erik Brynjolfsson and Andrew McAfee

The Great Restructuring is apparent to many who are engaged within and outside business enterprises. In addition to Erik Brynjolfsson and Andrew McAfee, authors such as Nilofer Merchant, Terri Griffith, Irene Ing, Linda Sanford, and Geoffrey Moore (all of whom are referenced in this book) are engaged in explorations of how to understand the rapid changes in the global economy and the emergence of new organizations, business models, and career paths.

Our small contribution to this exploration focuses on the customer experience. It has become clear to every business that customer relationships are changing quickly and massively in the digital era. Customers become frustrated, and migrate to disruptive offerings. Many large established businesses, abandoned by good customers, face stasis, low employee morale, and a dismal future.

Much of the problem stems from the failure of enterprises to serve customers as individuals. Businesses deal in aggregations, because aggregation is deemed necessary to realize efficiencies. They can monitor and manage segments, geographies, service lines, and brands, but not so much individuals. Yet the underlying trend in the digital revolution that is bringing about the Great Restructuring points toward the individualization of opportunity. Individuals can exchange information about their behaviors, preferences, values, and needs for a personalized service response delivered on a platform of their choosing. Moreover, businesses deal in objective outputs. Even though they are migrating from the product-centric world to the service-centric world, they continue to measure outputs. But the output of service is a customer experience, subjectively and idiosyncratically evaluated. This creates a new and different challenge for business strategists.

Old strategy tools wedded to legacy data, processes, and technologies are hindering rapid, intelligent, individualized response. Fortunately, there is an emerging alternative we propose, with the potential to change every aspect of business strategy.

Service and Service Science

The context within which our exploration takes place is the radical re-invention of value creation that is under way in the global economy, via the interaction of two vectors of change. First, the majority of value creation now occurs in services, and all economies are moving in the direction of an increase in the percentage of GDP generated by the services component.

Second, a large and increasing proportion of services are digital, that is, they are delivered digitally, involve some form of a digital interface, and are intermediated via digital technology, or both, often via a Cloud platform.

Service Science is an emerging field that strives to bring together many disciplines (computer science, information systems and technology, cognitive science, economics, organizational behavior, human resources

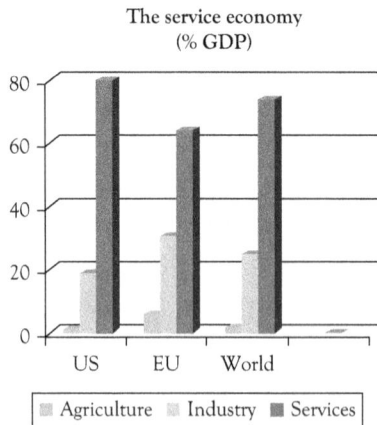

Figure 1. Service component of economies.[2]

management, marketing, operations research, and others) in an attempt to study and understand service systems.[3]

Service Thinking

Service Thinking is a business model that derives from Service Science. It is the systemic application to the enterprise of a seven-point framework, which we introduce here for the first time, to establish the globally integrated service standard, and to identify the pathways to transformational service innovation and absolute competitive advantage.

The Impact of Service Thinking on Enterprise Transformation

Service Thinking offers new practical adaptations of business informatics that will transform enterprise design. New challenges are presented, such as new roles for provider and customer in value creation, the qualitative, subjective, and idiosyncratic nature of the customer experience, and new realizations of value in the form of value-in-experience and value-in-context. The enterprise must be re-engineered, including business architecture, resource allocation, and metrics. Engineers, specifically, who are designing service delivery via digital technologies, must be cognizant of the Service Thinking framework in designing for customer acceptance.

No framework or approach currently exists to design such enterprise responses, although there are partial contributions from multiple sources, including academic research, business research, computer science, analytics, and finance. The synthesis we propose is new. The result is a uniquely adaptive non-linear approach, with the potential to catalyze innovative new service initiatives.

The Service Thinking Brand

Our Service Thinking framework is a new brand of strategic modeling for business. It challenges conventional strategic practice. In that spirit, we offer the following Challenger Brand Manifesto.[4]

The Service Thinking Manifesto

Core insight: It's clear to every business that their customer relationships are changing quickly and massively in the digital era. But old strategy tools wedded to established technologies are getting in the way of rapid and intelligent response. Customers become frustrated, and migrate to disruptive offerings. Businesses, abandoned by good customers, face stasis, low employee morale and a dismal future. Fortunately, there is an emerging alternative based on Service Thinking, with the potential to change every aspect of business strategy.			
Core belief: Service thinking, with customer co-creation at its core, opens new paths to accelerated growth through the emergent strategy of individualized service.	**Change Impact:** Replaces prescriptive strategy tools and a process-based concrete-pouring of enterprise technologies.	**Core offer:** New growth via re-thinking the enterprise system of value creation with the 7-point Service Thinking framework	**Brand behavior:** Liberating enterprises, management, employees and resources to serve the individualized needs of customers.
Who are our customers and how will we make them feel? Business leaders, liberated by the collaborative energy of Service Thinking.		Ideas/actions/language • Current state assessment/future state potential • 7-point Service Thinking framework service as experience • Co-creation within service ststems • Modular business architecture/ componentization • Run-transform-innovate • Global-mobile-social scalable platforms • Multisided metrics	

We are not the first to think this way. Prescient business writers such as Richard Normann foresaw emergent strategy as design and redesign of business systems.

> In so volatile a competitive environment, strategy is no longer a matter of positioning a fixed set of activities along a value chain. Increasingly, successful companies do not just *add* value, they *reinvent* it. Their focus of strategic analysis is not the company or even the industry but the *value-creating system* itself, within which different economic actors—suppliers, business partners, allies, customers—work together to *co-produce* value. Their key strategic task is the *reconfiguration* of roles and relationships among this constellation of actors in order to mobilize the creation of value in new forms and by new players. And their underlying strategic goal is to create an ever-improving fit between competencies and customers. To put it another way, successful companies conceive of strategy as systematic social innovation: *the continuous design and redesign of complex business systems.*[5]

We believe the journey of continuous design and redesign of complex business systems can be guided by the North Star called Service, and propelled by the motivation to serve the individual customer.

What Exactly Is Service Thinking? Where Does it Lead Us?

Service Thinking hinges on two overarching changes in the digital economy: (1) the relationship between provider and customer has changed dramatically and continues to evolve; (2) the design of enterprise operations to serve this new customer relationship is dramatically different from previous business architecture:

1. The change in the provider–customer relationship is driven by the unique customer dynamics of service:

   1.1 The output of service is an experience, which is subjectively evaluated by the customer. Vargo & Lusch' Service-Dominant Logic (S-D Logic) Fundamental Proposition (FP) 10 states that value is uniquely and phenomenologically determined by the beneficiary. Since no two customers perceive and feel in the same way, and since individual customers perceive and feel differently in different times, locations, and contexts, service delivery is driven remorselessly toward individualization and personalization. The economics of individualization is evolving rapidly. Starbucks customizes its service and provides the experience of community; they offer much more than just coffee.

   1.2 Now experiences are co-created. A service provider can only create a value proposition. S-D Logic FP 7 states that the enterprise cannot deliver value, but only offer value propositions. Not until the customer responds to the proposition by committing resources (e.g. in an information exchange) is experiential value created. Enterprises must elevate their skills in co-creation. Zipcar is a good example of a car as service to urban dwellers and provides specialization and integration into the offerings of a complex city transportation system.

1.3 The service experience is never a result of a one-on-one relationship between providers and customers. Spohrer et. al. (2012) state that service in context is always part of a dynamic ecology of evolving nested, network service system entities, providers, customers, authorities, and competitors. Customers constantly assemble and reassemble a set of service offerings in a service system to best meet their goal. They discard weak links and add new offerings with which they can create new value. Providers must fit in to customers' service system and prove they provide new value to replace or supplement existing components. For example, banking services must fit in to customers' life context of working, travelling, and using mobile devices in an unfettered way in any location.

2. Service providers have four ways to respond to the change in the customer relationship:

2.1 Business architecture and organization: Providers can best respond to the dynamics of co-creation and continuously evolving service systems via a componentized business architecture. Pohle et. al. (2005) and Moore (2011) state that outsourcing non-core components of the enterprise can free up needed resources to innovate specialized, and differentiated enterprise components. Weak links must be replaced with best practice service components from external partners. Strong components must be honed to absolute advantage. The internal and external components must be tightly integrated.

2.2 Scalable Glo-Mo-So platforms: Customers increasingly plug in to platforms that are global, mobile, and social for their service experience. Spohrer and Engelbart (2004) and Spohrer & Maglio (2006) state that individuals, enterprises and institutions augment their performance via a technology-enabled bootstrapping and continuous improvement processes that can co-elevate customer-provider service interactions through technology platforms. Providers must integrate with these global platforms for delivery, and embrace the social and mobile functions that are key to knowledge sharing and to scale.

2.3 Reallocation of resources (R-T-I): The dynamics of co-creation and service systems require continuous innovation. Sanford and Taylor (2005) state that entities (individuals, enterprises and institutes) must "let go to grow." Moore (2011) adds this discipline of letting go of the past can help "free your company's future from the pull of the past." The fiercest competitors find ways to reduce the cost of running today's business ("R") in order to transform ("T"), and innovate ("I") in offering new value propositions for Customers.

2.4 Metrics: Service Thinking metrics provide better ways to gauge success. Kumar et. al. (2007) state that "value merchants" systematically derive meaningful key performance indicators for multiple stakeholders directly and indirectly connected via value proposition networks. Multisided metrics systems measure customer sentiment, non-customer stakeholder sentiment, and the attitude of authorities, as well as the output growth of the Provider.

Taken together Service Thinking is the systemic application of these concepts to the enterprise to establish and identify the pathways to transformational and disruptive service innovation.

Service Thinking and The Individualization of Opportunity

The driving energy for economic growth comes from the individualization of opportunity.

Each of us as individuals seeks to improve our own quality of life. That is the purpose of all human action, as suggested by Ludwig von Mises.[6] When we serve, we exert our effort and apply our resources for the benefit of others, to improve their lives. The utility of human action is multiplied. The individual improves the quality of life of others at the same time as improving his/her own, in an ascending cycle of value co-creation that embraces enterprises, systems, cities, nations, and the planet.

The keys are (a) individualization organized within service systems combined with (b) specialization and integration. These two forces inexorably and irresistibly power the digital economy. The drive for continuous improvement and absolute advantage demands specialization—becoming better and better at serving the individual customer as a result of more and more specialized knowledge. Ultimately, this leads to individualization and personalization.

The drive for more and more complex and comprehensive systems—in healthcare, energy, transportation, finance, government—demands integration: the networking and knowledge sharing of systems nested in systems nested in even bigger systems. This sounds the death knell for the vertically integrated, self-sustaining enterprise that dominated the global economy in the second half of the 20th century. There is no better example of this than the extraordinary transformation of IBM from being the dominant computing-business-machines-company-serving-industry to becoming the leading orchestrator of data integration and smarter services for sectors that include healthcare, transportation, and many other private and public domains.

Service Thinking can translate to individual opportunity as well. The individual, by developing specialized knowledge, has the opportunity to contribute at any level to any system through integration. This can be as a one-person application designer in a smartphone service system, or an employee-by-choice making a unique contribution to a team project within an enterprise engaged in service, or a government worker who chooses to contribute to service in a civic system of city, region, or national governance.

Individuals can choose and design how to serve and contribute through the Service Thinking framework. If they choose to serve in a large enterprise, they will measure their contribution through a lens of evaluation that is more multifaceted than ever before. They may design their own engagement, and generate their own motivations.

If they choose to serve as single-employee enterprises or small start-ups or local service businesses, they may evaluate their contribution in equally varied terms, in how they serve the needs of customers, community, and other stakeholders.

The individualization of opportunity opens up vast new horizons of personal contribution and global growth. Service Thinking is its manifesto.

The Service Thinking Revolution Will Be in the Hands of Entrepreneurs and Regional Small- and Medium-Sized Enterprises (RSME)

The individualization of opportunity coupled with scalable platforms for the delivery of service will open up new growth energy. Historically, capital allocation has been undemocratic. It has favored large businesses with institutional access to investment capital, or, alternatively, a highly selected group of start-ups with relationship access to pools of venture capital. The Service Thinking future will be much more democratic.

Sramana Mitra, founder of the global incubator 1M/1M, is an evangelist for global entrepreneurs to use the bandwidth connectivity to access online learning, online access to capital, and online channels to build businesses. She states:

If we can democratize the education and incubation of entrepreneurs on a global scale, I believe that it would not only check the infant entrepreneur mortality, it would create a much more stable economic system.

Why? Because this middle of the pyramid—large numbers of small and medium businesses—is outside the reach of the speculators. If they produce something of value that their customers want, they can build stable businesses. They may not grow 300% a year. They may never become billion dollar enterprises.[7]

That's Okay.

Too much energy in the business world today is being spent on high-growth businesses that go after very large business opportunities. All of the startup incubation eco-system of the world focuses on the venture-fundable businesses only. As a result, less than 1% of the world's entrepreneurs are able to access high caliber incubation support.

My thesis is that the other 99% entrepreneurs hold the key to Capitalism 2.0: a system of distributed, democratic capitalism. Still focused on creating value, generating wealth, creating jobs, but not so focused on speculation.

Let's Get Started

We have organized this book to explain and illustrate our Service Thinking framework for use by any business or enterprise of any size to increase opportunities. We emphasize that our approach is non-linear, and can be hinged in multiple ways. Nevertheless, a book requires a starting point, and we begin with the most important insights: value is created through the customer experience and the co-creation of value is the key to opening the portals to opportunity and growth.

CHAPTER 1

Service Thinking Will Transform 21st Century Business

The digital revolution is far more significant than the invention of writing or even of printing.

—Douglas Engelbart

We propose and support a prodigious claim: Service Thinking is a new approach to business that will change virtually every aspect of creating and sustaining enterprises. Specifically, these changes will impact the:

- fundamental nature of the relationship between the provider and the customer;
- role of the employee;
- basic functioning of the front end of the enterprise: marketing, sales, and delivery;
- enterprise approach to strategy;
- organization of the entire enterprise;
- operational infrastructure;
- governance of resource allocation; and
- enterprise definition and measurement of success.

Service Thinking is the framework for this new approach to value creation in the digital economy, with transformative implications for the future of business, work, careers, and creation of wealth in the 21st century. Importantly, the transformation will enable both great economic growth and improved quality of life.

IBM, one of the largest, most successful Global Corporations, provides an example of the transformative power of actively applying Service Thinking for societal impact and healthy business growth as measured by every important financial metric. IBM's profits in 2010 were $13.06 per share, compared with $3.07 in 2001. Return on equity was 70% in 2010 compared with 16% in 2001.[1] The company achieved 31 straight quarters of revenue and profit growth, and $6.2 billion in productivity improvements in 2005–2009. IBM achieved growth in both developed and emerging markets. The company believes that "The single greatest contributor to global economic and enterprise growth will be Service Science. Computer Science took us to annual revenues of $100 billion and Service Science and Smarter Systems will take us to $200 billion.[2]"

Other companies large and small, well-known and (as yet) unknown are adopting their own versions of Service Thinking. Some of them we will highlight in this book and on our website. Service Thinking will improve outcomes for a wide range of constituencies:

- Enterprises that can implement Service Thinking
- Executives trained and skilled in Service Thinking
- Universities with the specialized knowledge and capabilities for service science education
- Students certified in Service Thinking
- Entrepreneurs who want to start and accelerate a business
- National, regional, and municipal governments that can better understand their ecosystem and use technology to improve their economy, services, and quality of life

Service Thinking will change careers. Professionals who understand and are skilled in Service Thinking will lead and be in great demand.

What Is Service?

Let's begin by defining service with a different interpretation than most of us are familiar with:

Service is a form of value creation. A service provider invests time, money, and effort into developing a deep understanding of a customer's needs. Based on this resource of understanding, the provider constructs a value proposition promising to improve the customer's current experience. The customer transforms the proposition into shared value by responding—sharing information on their perception of the experience. The relationship now *co-evolves*, and the provider and customer co-develop processes that enable a shared service experience. The ongoing engagement provides more information to deepen the provider's understanding and further improve the value proposition. Both then *co-elevate*—the provider and customer continuously and iteratively improve the value proposition to bring the co-creation of value to a higher level with shared experience and a pool of shared knowledge. The value from this extended relationship is realized over time and monetized through transactions in the applicable business model.

This definition has important implications: it is a two-way relationship, based on an understanding of needs; it is an engagement over time; it co-evolves and co-elevates, with monetization not necessarily integral with service delivery. Google search is a good example. The service is delivered free. Customer engagement improves via satisfactory search results, resulting in a continuous improvement of the underlying algorithm. So, the service improves, leading to better customer experience. Monetization occurs in a separate business model: the delivery of advertising.

Our definition of service specifically includes the exchange of knowledge and information between the provider and the customer to co-evolve and co-elevate the relationship. This does not mean that customers must endlessly complete customer satisfaction forms to let providers know how to improve their value proposition. The customer enters into the information exchange—a "data deal"—voluntarily, knowing that the increasing amount and quality of data they share with the provider results in emergent improvements in a service experience tailored more precisely to their individual needs in the time and space of their choosing.

Irene Ng refers to the customer's contribution of information to service providers as "digital work" that customers perform as their contribution to the two-way service. They click on websites, tap mobile apps, or open and close the door of a refrigerator equipped with an information chip in the "Internet of things" and send information to the power company and the refrigerator manufacturer.[3] This is their "data deal"—the customer submits data through behavior in return for the anticipation of a more customized service experience. The data is created in use, and the provider has to be smart to gather, interpret, and act upon the aggregate of data from one and many customers.

What about products that are not digital or Internet delivered? Could a vending machine or a soft drink become a service? If The Coca-Cola Company just films you or collects sales data, there is no service. But if you press a button or scan a card in a vending machine, you could activate a service relationship. The provider, The Coca-Cola Company, could use the information to determine which flavors, sizes, and forms (diet or sugared for example) are best sellers or that you particularly like, and can change the offering to best customize it for the service user. You have entered the "data deal" and the potential of service is opened up.

What Is the Difference Between Service Science and Service Thinking?

Service Thinking has noble antecedents, one of which is Service Science, an interdisciplinary field that focuses on fundamental science, models, concepts, and applications to drive new value creation in services. It is a recognized field of research and education, with a 30-year history. Many universities around the globe have offered various courses and programs that provide the theoretical underpinnings for government, NGOs, and industry to apply innovation in service in a systematic way.

Service Thinking is Service Science applied in a practical, evidence-based way to create commercial value through the development of specialized knowledge and service competencies to create new and more profitable business growth, using processes, tools, and methods based on the underlying scientific rigor.

Service Thinking is following the footsteps of processes that enable us to understand how innovation may be applied to problems and opportunities through asking better questions, and using proven principles, tools, and methods, to co-create solutions. This contrasts with prescriptive model-based formulas and processes that are derived from overarching strategies developed from theories, but not co-created in practice.

Service Thinking Approach

We propose a systematic approach to Service Thinking that practitioners and system designers can apply. However, it is not a linear process. There are seven foundational concepts; the first three address how the customer is changing the nature of the relationship with providers, and the remaining four are adaptations initiated on the provider side. Any one of the seven can be the "entry point" to begin the service transformation, depending on the problem to be solved or the opportunity to be seized. Think of them as hinges that connect with one another in combinations rather than as separate or linear process steps.

Service Thinking challenges many conventional approaches to business, and one of them is the prescriptive model of strategy, which promises that businesses can identify and pursue the winning strategy if they analyze the right data sets in the right way using the right strategy tools from the right consultants. Service Thinking takes a more humble approach. Strategy is emergent—it co-evolves and co-elevates as a result of the relationship with customers within an ecosystem that is swirling with dynamic, nonlinear and unpredictable change. The skill for successful business managers becomes *orchestration*—the ability to identify and connect a wide variety of players and offerings and arrange them into a winning and continuously improving value proposition.

The Service Thinking Framework

The goal in applying these seven concepts of Service Thinking is to move the enterprise toward customer value co-creation readiness.

The Output of Service Is an Experience

We have been trained to believe that we live in a world of objectivity. The dominant mindset is scientific. We believe that business is like science, that we can run experiments, observe the results, and develop objective measurements. The outputs of business, in this scientific world, are all objective and can be stated as numbers and captured as data. In service, however, the output is intangible and subjective. The output of service is

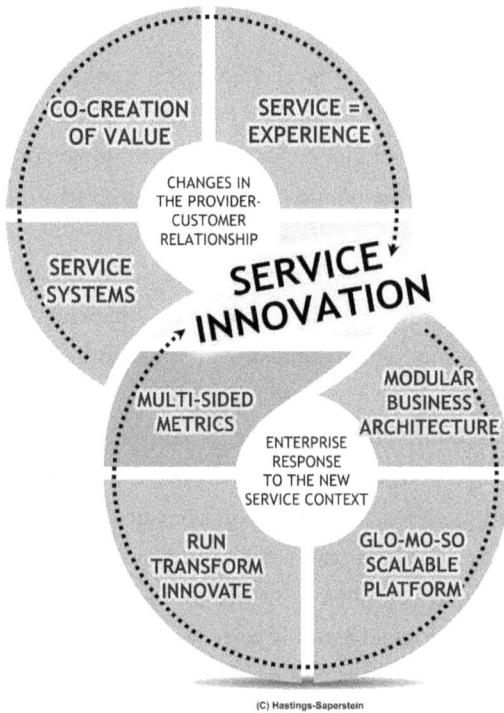

Figure 1.1. The Service Thinking framework.

an experience. Only the customer can determine whether the experience is positive or negative, and if it meets expectations or fails to do so. That determination is emotional—it's a feeling on the part of the customer. And it can vary—depending on the customer's mood, on context, on culture, and on many other variables, some identifiable, some not. Service Thinking recognizes that we are entering an era of subjectivity.

Customer experience is the conjunction of all experiences a consumer has with an enterprise over the duration of their relationship.[4] Organizations may have deep gaps in dealing with their own customers because of multiple channels of engagement with the same customer. This trend leads organizations to revisit some of their core capabilities and competences in customer engagement. In North America, for example, 80% of clients are happy with their bank service; however, only 50% say they will remain with their current bank over the next 6 months. This reflects the finding that globally, only 42% of bank customers rate their experience as being positive. Furthermore, satisfaction levels with branches, despite being the most expensive and most developed channel, averages 40% world-wide with highest being 60% in North America.[5]

Transformative Effect

Everything we thought we knew about the scientific objectivity of business initiatives will be transformed into a new lexicon of customer subjectivity. Customer satisfaction must be re-defined for this new era. Defining, measuring, and addressing subjective phenomena will be the new source of business success.

Co-Creation of Value

Service is defined as an action of one individual or entity taken for the benefit of another individual or entity. The value output of a service offering is an *experience*—subjective and hard to measure. The customer is a co-provider of the service experience. The customer may participate enthusiastically, or may change his/her mind, withhold information, exercise subjective evaluations, or otherwise make delivery of the desired experience a challenge and hard to control. The employee, especially the front-line employee, has a major share of this co-production. The employee may have the skill, competence, and temperament to react creatively with the customer, or may be confused and confounded by the subjectivity of the interaction. The quality of the experience as perceived by the customer is affected by the employee's reaction, in real time.

The firm must design a service proposition that can be reliably delivered in this subjective arena of the potentially inconsistent interaction. The firm must provide services and a positive experience not only to the customer, but also to the employee, in forms such as training and a supportive environment that contributes to the employee's delivery capability to the customer. Capitalizing on this business imperative, the company Bunchball has built a successful business using big data and gamification to measure and enhance employee and customer engagement. Bunchball, founded by Rajat Paharia, is one of the companies profiled in this book.[6]

Increasingly, the deliverer of the service experience may be an app or an automated customer interaction tool. The principle of co-creation does not change—value is created only when the customer commits resources and effort to participate, and when the provider can demonstrate responsiveness to the customer's input. In this case, the engineering team is on the front-line of delivery, and must be able to see and understand the customer's input (including the emotional inputs of satisfaction or disappointment with the service experience), and be able to respond with service improvements.

Transformative Effect

The multidirectional services triad of customer, employee, and enterprise replaces the old one-way dyad of selling products to customers, with the customer in the role of the revenue source at the end of the value chain. *Value in experience* replaces *value in exchange*. This is the principle of co-creation of value.

Service Systems

Service is never one provider serving one customer. The customer assembles a service system to get a job done or meet a need. The provider assembles a service system to do that job or address that need. A service system is a combination of people, knowledge, technologies, and a value proposition. A simple example is healthcare. The patient and a primary care doctor co-create value in the form of superior health outcomes. Each is part of a much greater service system that supports their co-creation. The provider healthcare system includes other specialist doctors, nurses, information, technology, research, financial systems, hospitals, and medical equipment. The patient's service system includes family, information, diet, transportation, insurance, banking, and fitness equipment. The service system of the provider and the service system of the customer combine in a shared value co-creation network. Both the provider and the customer are continually rearranging their service systems, replacing some components with others to increase the value that is co-created. Service systems are dynamic and changing as they absorb the input of the co-creating customer. Businesses must study and understand the system—not just their own contribution to it—in order to succeed within it.

Transformative Effect

The enterprise must deliver not just value but *value in context*. To succeed, it is necessary to investigate and understand the customer's service system and prove the qualifications to fit in and contribute new value. Marketing is an example of a function that is transformed by this concept.

Modular Business Architecture

The assembly and refinement of service systems is a continuous search for the best co-creation partners. To qualify, businesses and individuals must specialize more to ensure absolute advantage and avoid replacement in the system; they will shed competencies in which they are not advantaged. This search for continued relevance and differentiation in the swirling dynamics of service systems and co-creation can be summarized in the phrase *specialization and integration*. Business modules must specialize—perhaps hyper-specialize is a better term—to maintain the knowledge edge that makes them the best. As specialists, they must integrate smoothly into the service system so that the customer experiences no friction. Just as service systems are composed of specialist modules, so business will become confederations of such specialized modules, loosely coupled as a single enterprise. We will refer to this phenomenon of business architecture later in this book as *componentization*.

Transformative Effect

Modular business architecture changes the way we think about organizational design and structure, including the role of processes and technology as organizational resources, as well as "insourcing" and "outsourcing." Start-up firms, especially, will find a new role as components in larger service systems.

Scalable Glo-Mo-So Platforms

How does specialization scale? A platform and set of enabling and implementing technologies are required to scale up the service system for global mass delivery, in such a way as to accommodate specialization and co-creation (get the "local" right) while creating scale efficiency (get the "global" right). To enable and implement the collaborative specializations inherent in co-creation, many of the technology tools are "social," both within the provider organization (collaboration around specialized knowledge and skills) and between the provider and the customer (collaboration around co-creation of the service experience). For a full and uninterrupted service experience, the tools must include mobile functionality. Think of UPS drivers and their mobile devices for recording a customer delivery. Thus, platforms for scaling up the service system are global-mobile-social.

Transformative Effect

All businesses will become social businesses. The traditional advantages of scale (e.g., market power from market share, procurement power through leveraging the size of the purchase order) are no longer broadly relevant.

Continuous Improvement via Learning

Continuous improvement is required to maintain the service system, sharpen the specialization, integrate new ideas, and retain competitive advantage. Therefore, resources must be shifted and re-allocated toward learning. A useful term for this process is the *Run-Transform-Innovate* ratio (R-T-I). Running the system must be efficient, but minimal resources should be required; more resources must be allocated to transformation (making the current system ever more efficient and lower cost) and innovation (replacing the current system with a new, disruptive and superior one). Service Thinking companies constantly review their R-T-I investment ratios. Are they paying enough critical attention to the running of the everyday business operation to ensure efficiency? Are they always seeking ways to transform those operations to find new opportunities for efficiency? And are they investing in the R&D to innovate, that is, create new revenue and profit streams that might potentially make the current operations obsolete?

Transformative Effect

Traditional management governance models to promote continuity and smoothness of business progression are replaced by new governance models promoting as much dynamic change as possible and allocating resources accordingly.

Multisided Metrics

When value is co-created, metrics center on the outcomes of co-creation rather than the one-sided financial metrics of provider revenues and profits. Service quality is a multisided metric—it requires the provider to measure quality and the customer to report their experience. Customer loyalty is similarly multisided. Such metrics are often time-released and not limited to the moment of the interaction, forcing business to re-think the periodicity of annual results, quarterly earnings, and other such time-bound metrics. In large service systems, the outcomes are world-changing and quality-of-life enhancing (Smarter Planet, Smarter Cities, Smarter Workforce, Smarter Education, etc.). In smaller systems, the outcomes can be just as world-changing: a healthier population around a local community health system, or a more entrepreneurial, innovative, and employment-ready body of young people from a university.

Transformative Effect

The traditional metrics of business will be replaced by new metrics of shared value creation, co-elevation, and sustainability. Multisided metrics will need to be applied to non-customer stakeholders (such as regulators/NGOs) and those who report on/criticize/advocate in the new media environment, including the blogosphere. Consider the impact on the brands whose outsourced garment manufacturing workers are mistreated (in the subjective view of commentators) by sub-contractors in developing countries; metrics need to be able to account for this reputation risk.

Service Thinking in Action

Let's see how the seven concepts work in the "real world" through two different case examples: Cloud Computing and Starbucks.

Case Study: Cloud Computing

The dramatic and high impact switch in the technology sector from installed IT systems to cloud computing is a current example of the massive change that is inherent in the ideas of Service Thinking.

For decades, IT systems for large enterprises have been in "product mode" rather than "service mode." The customer experience of dealing with a provider who is in product mode has been characterized by a number of dominant attributes:

- The enterprise makes a major commitment to the IT systems supplier and pays largely upfront for hardware, software, installation, and customization.
- Often, such as when changing or upgrading systems, the enterprise must change its internal working processes, retrain employees, and, generally, commit to a significant amount of internal organizational and infrastructure change.
- Large amounts of time pass between the commitment to the new system and when it becomes operational. Delays and cost overruns can be quite common.
- Complexity is inherent, and it is well-documented that only a small percentage of the capabilities of IT systems that they purchase are actually utilized by most enterprises.
- There is supplier "lock-in"—it is high-risk to change from one vendor to another once an enterprise has made the commitment to the system.

Cloud computing is a Service Thinking approach to enterprise IT that is designed to address all of these experiential issues. For enterprise users of IT, the concept of cloud computing is that they no longer need to buy and install large complex systems locally at their own sites. Instead, they can draw down computing power and access and utilize software applications that are installed externally in large computing installations. Enterprises can purchase computing power and applications as units of usage—that is, operating expense or OpEx—rather than in the form of installed systems, that is, capital expense or CapEx. For example, Amazon sells cloud-based computing services by the hour, with a price list that ranges from $0.02 per hour to $2 per hour depending on the size, complexity, and CPU and memory usage of the particular instance of usage. Salesforce.com sells its CRM applications on a monthly basis, ranging from $5 per user per month to $250 per user per month. These prices can be expected to decline as scale increases and technology advances.

Enterprise computing is being transformed from a high cost, high complexity, pay-up-front product to a low price, variable cost service accessed on demand. This "service-ization" of computing brings with it enormous additional changes. Many of these changes are inherent in the Service Thinking paradigm for doing business in the service economy:

- *Risk in the business model is transferred from the purchaser to the provider.* In the case of cloud consulting, no longer is the enterprise required to commit up-front to the product and installation, and to pay well in advance of any usage of the system. Now, the enterprise can purchase computing when, and only when, it needs the service, and can switch suppliers with relative ease if the service is not working for them. The service provider takes the risk of building the remote computing installation, and designing, building, and testing software and making it market-ready before any cash flow comes their way. Risk transfer and the distribution of risk flexibility will be new variables for management and service designers to deal with in the service economy.
- *Unit pricing of service instances will tend to decline.* As more and more specialization in business architectures takes hold, and new entrants and innovators find new ways to deliver and to create demand for service instances, unit price competition will drive down unit prices. This is good news for the service customer and a big challenge for the service provider.
- *The route to building customer franchise value changes and requires new competencies.* In enterprise computing, customer franchise value was built by making a series of big one-time sales to large buyers. The shift to services changes the franchise value model to one of serial consumption of small units

of usage—such as a unit of computing power. The business competency required for success changes from the ability to make a big sale to the ability to create continuous demand for small increments of usage, to create incremental demand with premium services and options on each transaction, and to scale up by accumulating thousands or millions or billions of instances. Customer loyalty—in the context of low barriers to exit and shifting—is critical to customer franchise value. Zipcar is an example of a B2C relationship illustrating this principle. If you live in an urban center, renting a car by the day or hour makes sense as a component of your personal transportation service system.

- Demand creation—what we used to call marketing—is a more critical skill in the service economy than ever before. As we shall see, it takes new forms compared to traditional marketing.

- *As the influence of the end-user increases, user-level behavioral and attitudinal data become a powerful tool for service performance enhancement.* In many service industries, as customers co-create the desired service experience, their subjective perceptions of service quality and their individual usage decisions can make or break the service provider's success. Every micro-transaction can create behavioral data. Every perception shared on social media and recorded on a "How did we do?" query can produce sentiment data. When billions and trillions of these data points are created, it is called "Big Data." Applying analytics, businesses can understand why their customers behave the way they do, what motivates them, and (with predictive data modeling) what they are likely to do in the future. It is the service economy that creates the opportunity for big data and it is in the service economy where analytics can create the most value by helping businesses co-create better experiences.

Risk transfer from the customer to the provider, declining unit prices, the primacy of demand creation, and the analysis of detailed data to focus that demand creation—these are some of the attributes of the service economy that hold such promise. They all favor the customer, thereby creating more value, and lifting GDP. They all encourage innovation and entrepreneurship on the supply side, improving economic efficiency and generating economic growth. Service science is an exacting discipline, but promises a route to new revenue and growth opportunities.

Case Study: Starbucks

Walk into a Starbucks store in Hong Kong, Hartlepool, or Hoboken, and you can co-create your desired experience in a pretty much identical form. You'll encounter the same smiling faces of well-trained baristas and service staff. You'll probably see some familiar fixtures like espresso making machinery, chalkboard messages, eco-friendly napkins, and available Wi-Fi. You can use the shared language you've adopted for descriptions of drinks and sizes of cups. You can expect the same taste experience, and you can probably also explore some local specialties and innovations.

Starbucks is global, social, and mobile. It is global in the sense that you can find Starbucks in many of the highly developed urban centers of the world, on multiple continents, and in multiple countries. The value proposition for Starbucks stores is global: a "third place" for customers between home and office, to which you can feel free to come at any time, stay as long as you want, connect with the world, and do whatever you like, on your own or with friends. Starbucks Chairman Howard Schultz calls it "Human Connection."[7] Note that this value proposition is clearly a service and does not even mention a product like coffee.

It is social in many ways, the primary one being that it is a place to connect with others—in-person, online, or by phone. The stores offer Wi-Fi so that customers can be connected. They generate a lot of social media activity from their customers: I am at Starbucks; meet me there! Starbucks offers online special offers (your own birthday invitation to celebrate with a free beverage) and encourages online community chats and sharing so it is more than just a social gathering place.

It's mobile in the sense that it caters to the mobile customer. Their peripatetic, always-connected, always-on customer base knows the pleasure of dropping in, signing on, doing work, holding a quick meeting, touching base with friends, or simply refreshing while on the go. Your mobile device can locate a Starbucks near to wherever you happen to be.

Starbucks is also an exercise in continuous co-creation. An order for a "Vente skinny non-caf latte, no foam, extra hot" is an audible expression of the customer adapting to the provider's flexible value proposition to match his/her own individual preferences. Starbucks gets it right globally and gets it right locally. This is the essence of a scalable global service delivery.

Starbucks exhibits all the principles of service science at work in the B2C sector:

1) Service as experience

Starbucks is not in the coffee business, in the sense of coffee as a product. Starbucks is in the experience business. The experience for the customer is a life-enhancing one. Customers feel better about a life that includes the experience of passing through the Starbucks drive-in window on the way to work and anticipating the indulgence of enjoying the highest quality, individually specified beverage at an office desk. They feel good about being part of the Starbucks community, meeting people at the Starbucks location, and finding a welcoming and familiar-feeling Starbucks store in cities they have never been to before. They feel good about a company that has a social conscience and acts upon it. Feelings are what Starbucks produces.

2) Co-creation of value

The first rung of the co-creation ladder is the system Starbucks has designed for customers to co-create value in the products they order and how they order them. Using standard components such as cup sizes, varieties of coffee beans, a few liquids (water, milk, and soy milk), a few additives (cream, whipped cream, caramel sauce, and flavorings), temperature (hot, extra-hot, and iced), the provider enables the customer to combine preferences in a way that feels customized and made-to-order.

A second rung of co-creation lies in location options. "Do you want that here or to-go?" You can sit at a table or at a bar by the window or outside, or in an easy chair. Or you can take your Starbucks to your car, bus, or office. You can use the drive-through window and never leave your car.

A third rung is provided in the form of accompaniments offered alongside beverages, a portfolio that Starbucks has expanded and refined over time. You can buy a cookie or a banana, a fruit snack or popcorn, a sandwich (hot or cold—the temperature option, again) or a bistro box.

Innovation is also co-created. The customer can provide two forms of input. One is behavior—what do they buy most, which products have the most loyalty, what patterns can reveal insights (e.g., which accompaniments are used most with hot drinks and which with cold), how are weekend behaviors different than weekday behaviors. These behavioral observations are captured in data streams created via the checkout register and can be linked to individuals via smart cards. The second input is opinion which can be expressed directly in response to queries on a website, or indirectly through e-mails, blogs, and social media commentary, which Starbucks can analyze for sentiment trends. As service providers become more sophisticated in the gathering and analysis of these customer inputs, the old form of market research (asking questions in reaction to artificial stimulus) will disappear. Innovation will cease to take the form of new ideas created by the provider to be "tested" for customer acceptance. Innovation will become the intelligent listening to customer signals provided by behavioral observations and sentiment analysis.

3) Service system

What is the job that customers are hiring Starbucks to help them get done? We can define it as refreshment and relaxation with others. Perhaps we can associate that job with a particular time of day—morning, noon, evening, and breaks in between those time milestones—and often integrated with other tasks such as working on a laptop or digitally communicating with others. We could also say that the job requires the service delivery to fit in to another activity—for example, on the way to work, or close to the office or school at break time.

To get this job done, a customer requires a service system that extends beyond Starbucks. Transportation is involved, whether driving, riding the bus or train, or biking, or walking. For those who consume Starbucks beverages while driving or riding in a car, the service system has made this easier by providing beverage holders as part of car design. Parking may be required, often provided by a mall operator or landlord, or local government authority. The customer might include third-party information in their service system, such as dietary guidelines, or friends' recommendations on their social network. For those customers who want to catch up on news, they might bring a newspaper or iPad into their service system. Starbucks service must fit into the customer's service system and make a contribution to improving its performance. The cups must fit the beverage holders in the car, parking must be convenient, there must be a place to read and Wi-Fi should be nice. *Fitting in* and *contributing* are the new pillars of marketing to a customer's service system where co-creation takes place.

On the provider side, Starbucks must assemble the best service system to get the right coffee, liquids, machines, temperature management, sandwiches and snacks, and containers to the store at the right time. They must hire people who can co-create the Starbucks experience by cheerily and speedily delivering the customized co-created beverage and experience. They must develop the analytics capability to listen and respond to consumer sentiment and to observe and translate customer behavioral patterns. They must install Wi-Fi networks. They might go further and curate some digital content that's unique to Starbucks and consumed on a visit to the store. The provider service system is dynamic, constantly changing in response to the signals from user behavior and sentiment. Assembling this *shared value network* in support of the value proposition is the core competency of the service provider.

4) Modularized business architecture

To illustrate this principle through the lens of Starbucks, we can start by listing the competencies that are required for the service system we described above. These might include production of input materials (like coffee), procurement of those materials (contracting, purchasing, shipping and logistics, quality control), real estate management (locational skills, leasing, legal), store design, technology (espresso machines to Wi-Fi routers, GPS locating software for store locator plug-ins), hiring, training, management, and motivation of service personnel, communications (advertising, surface design, website design, and maintenance), data collection and metrics. There could be a much longer list, depending on what level of detail we choose to go to. Starbucks then decides which of these competencies it should develop in-house because they are critical to success and best performed by Starbucks itself for reasons of absolute advantage (we do it better than anyone else could) and control. Competencies that don't qualify become areas of external specialization—to whom should we entrust this competency and how do we integrate with them. Growing coffee, for example, is a competency best left to skilled and experienced farmers. Starbucks must decide how to contract with them and manage the quality and consistency of supply from these external specialists, apart from supplying them with specialized information (training and expertise) to produce better outputs and stronger relationships.

In a service system, it is critical that this business architecture of internal and external specialization is carefully and rigorously designed and executed, and constantly reviewed and refined. The successful service system is a confederation of specialized competency modules, constantly being reviewed by customers to evaluate whether each competency is the best of all choices.

5) Scalable glo-mo-so platform

We usually think of enabling platforms in IT terms—hardware and software and data flows. For our current example, however, we can think of the enabling platform in a different way. For Starbucks, it is the organizational template of people and processes (OpEx), plus the specialized inputs and the physical plant (CapEx) that combines to enable service delivery on a global scale with local customization. To open a Starbucks in a new city is to implement a local instance of this global template. It would be possible to reproduce a San Francisco Starbucks in Safi or Saga by drawing from the template. Same physical footprint, same blueprint for water and electricity provision, same counter and sitting area design, same furniture, same machinery, same hiring screens, same training, and same cups. Same value proposition. Local management can then quickly and easily make local adjustments via an approach that provides flexibility within the template, defining what's fixed and must not change, and what's flexible and can be adapted locally.

6) *Continuous improvement via learning*

Starbucks uses customer feedback and learning to refine the running of the operation. Chairman Howard Schultz is famous for having re-focused the organization on basics like barista training, the time taken to complete a basic operation like making a latte, and the visibility of cafeteria operations to the customer. Transformations include further refinements of the operations (such as K-Cups and espresso machines for customers' home use and the addition of iced drinks). Innovations include Starbucks becoming a music store, an online content aggregator, a purveyor of food for meals as well as beverages and snacks, even experimenting with alcoholic beverages. Resources are allocated to these transformations and innovations by continuously increasing the efficiency of the "Run" part of the business—more automation in beverage preparation, more efficient supply networks, better training for coffee growers so that they raise the quality of the inputs.

Continuous learning through experimentation and customer co-creation is a mark of the service science enterprise.

7) *Multisided metrics*

How does Starbucks' approach utilize multisided metrics? The front page of the 2011 Annual Report focuses on building "a great enduring company"—a long-term view that balances "profitability and a social conscience." The document goes on to list a wide variety of metrics, including these:[8]

- Financial metrics: highest annual revenue ever ($US11.7B). Record operating margins and EPS.
- Global growth metrics: opened 900th store in Japan and 500th in Latin America; entered three new markets.
- Customer measures: served nearly 60 million customers per week (a measure of frequency); reached two million Gold Card members (a measure of loyalty).
- Environmental measures: reducing environmental impact, ethical sourcing.

- Community contribution measures: Create jobs for USA initiative, The Starbucks Foundation's funding to small companies and community businesses.

Starbucks' outcome is an enduring, growing enterprise that co-creates value for its shareholders, its customers, its partner communities, and its environment. Such a richly woven mosaic of outcome metrics is reflective of the business revolution of service science. Because co-creation of value is foundational, metrics must take account of all sides of the co-creation collaboration. Because value is co-created in a service system, metrics must monitor the strength and health of the whole system, not just the provider's singular role.

That is why businesses today must emphasize and measure their community and environmental activities. To thrive in a service system, enterprises must both fit in and contribute to that system. Contributions must accommodate not only shareholders and customers, but also the wider membership of the service system. How enterprises treat their non-customers is an important element in the perceptions of the enterprise held by customers, and therefore to the enduring strength of the brand.

CHAPTER 2

Co-Creating Service-Experience Value

Quality in a service or product is not what you put into it. It is what the client or customer gets out of it.

—Peter Drucker

Service-as-experience and the customer co-creation of that experience represent the most impactful, paradigm-shifting elements of Service Thinking. They place the service provider and customer in a new relationship, with limitless ramifications for business strategy and newly expanded opportunities for shared value creation.

Value-in-Experience

Value is a concept with a long history in economics and business. If we are willing, for the purposes of narrative, to broad-brush a vast history of economic thought into a single paragraph, we can say that the concept of value-in-use can be traced back to Adam Smith.[1] What became known as *marginal utility theory* posited that value (i.e., a price greater than zero) is a function of how useful a product is to its purchaser. While very few of us would use the term *marginal utility* in conversation, we have probably internalized the concept of value-in-use in our thinking about how business works, how prices are established, and how customers make decisions.

But value-in-experience is a different concept entirely. Services are not consumed; they are experienced. That is why we use the term customer in Service Thinking, not consumer. Consumption implies the destruction of value (once something is consumed it can't be consumed a second time). In the subjective world of experience, value is not something that is consumed in use. It is an emotion that is triggered in the mind of a customer as a result of a subjective judgment of how they feel as a result of participating in a service exchange.

Our economist of choice in defining value-in-experience is Ludwig Von Mises.[2] His focus on individual motivation—the goal of improving one's situation based on one's own individual context, values, and subjectively perceived needs—places him and his school in the forefront of Service Thinking. The fundamental idea that forms the basis of what von Mises called "praxeology"—and today many call behavioral economics—is that the world is the way it is as a result of individual human actions that rest on subjectively-made personal decisions. Humans act with a purpose; they act in order to achieve a desired state that they feel is preferable to their current state. In Service Thinking, we often call this purpose a response to a Need. Von Mises proposed a simple way to think of it: that every one of us has a little voice inside our head saying, "Life could be better if…"

When a customer chooses to hail a taxi to get to an appointment, he or she is thinking that "life could be better if" I experience the greater comfort and reduced stress of riding in the back of a cab rather than driving myself or taking public transportation. It is not an economic calculation of cost-per-mile or cost-per-minute, or a value comparison of alternative transportation systems. It is the decisive emotion that they will feel better as a result of the taxi experience than with the experience of fighting traffic and congestion and parking difficulties as a self-driver or with the experience of queuing and jostling with other commuters in the crowded confines of the bus or subway.

The key phrase is, "My life could be a little better."

If businesses put the customer experience at the forefront of their thinking—if they make the analysis of customer experience the first order of business rather than an after-the-fact review once the service is delivered—they will open up the opportunity to create new service innovations. Flywheel is an example of a start-up company that was built on the analysis of customer experience and the identification of a service experience gap. Continuing with the taxi example, Flywheel identified that the experience of hailing a taxi can generate some negative feelings. During busy times, the customer might be standing on the sidewalk waving their arms in vain because passing taxis are full. Someone on the other side of the street might pre-empt them by successfully hailing what they thought was "my taxi." There might be a long wait before successfully engaging a taxi, imposing stress and frustration onto the original decision to take a cab which was intended expressly to avoid those emotions. Flywheel enables customers to communicate their decision to take a cab via the touchscreen of an iPhone, which will quickly identify that a taxi is nearby, including the specific taxi number, and how long it will take to arrive, and (ultimately) that it has arrived. The customer can pay with the iPhone too, using a digital payment system. The frustration and stress are removed. The technology is not new (it combines—through API integration—iPhone touchscreen technology, Google maps, GPS, and the existing in-cab communication network) but the service is a disruptive breakthrough in the taxi service business. It makes the customer's life better.

The identification of value-in-experience is the first step in service innovation.

Co-Creation of Value

The second part of service innovation is the co-creation of value. Co-creation of value challenges our conventional thinking in these ways:

- Value itself is not inherent in products or services. There is no meaning in the concept of "value added."
- Co-creation of value requires new skills; individuals on the front-line of service delivery (or individual engineers and teams designing service delivery software) become far more important to the success of the enterprise.
- Innovation can no longer be approached as an internal enterprise process; the focus must be shifted entirely to an external activity with customers.
- The path to customer loyalty takes new directions and changes the basic ideas of marketing.

Success in this new context will require evidence-based thinking by enterprise leaders who understand that building a financially and socially sustainable business will require different business architecture for customer value co-creation. Business organization will change: traditional corporate divisions and standard business units (SBUs) are obsolete. Business strategy will change: Service Thinking includes a redefinition of business strategy from prescriptive to emergent. The role of IT changes to become a flexible, on-demand customer-responsive delivery system, as well as a source of customer understanding through analytics. There are new roles for employees.

A New Way of Thinking About Value

We tend to think of value as inherent in a business offering. A car has value, a Nike shoe has value, a credit card service from American Express has value, and a maintenance agreement with Hewlett Packard has value.

We must change this thinking. There is no inherent value in the product or offering. When it sits in inventory, it has no value (even though accounting principles allocate some numerical value to it based on either historical cost or projected future revenue from a sale).

Value is co-created by the provider and the customer. Both are required to contribute and participate. Value goes beyond the transaction. Value must be derived in the experience of the product or service. It is value-in-experience, not the inherent value. Value-in-experience is dynamic, sometimes subjective, and variable. It depends significantly on the perception of the customer. If the customer is enjoying a leisurely day, he/she may stand happily in the line reading e-mail on a smartphone while waiting for the Starbucks order to be delivered. If the customer is in a great hurry, he/she may be disappointed with the same time period for order fulfillment and may consider it sluggish service. A higher value is created in the first instance than in the second. If the customer has a series of bad days, he/she may find the Starbucks service design to be inadequate to meet their changing needs, even though that service design has been executed with consistency and exactitude.

The output of service design is a perceived customer experience. The quality of the customer experience is defined by the customer's feelings; the perception of the experience is subjective.

For exactly the same measured physical service delivery (the coffee arrived in 1 minute and 37 seconds, at a temperature of 170°F, with perfectly consistent taste characteristics resulting from a standardized, automated process), the customer's individual context will determine perception.

Experience Gap Analysis Can Free Us from Measurement-Based Mediocrity

Subjectivity is hard for us to deal with (or measure), because we have been trained for decades to be objective in business. Variability injects itself via the subjective customer experience, when we have been trained to eliminate variability as waste and inefficiency. This is the built-in mind-set of the industrial economy, which now is a legacy conceptual constraint. Standards should be more flexible, while we have been trained that, in order to scale, we must implement standards consistently. Scaling with capacity for variability is a powerful success factor in the cloud-based economy. Scaling to match consistent norms inhibits innovation.

For example, measurement that focuses on the size of the audience for commercial TV has resulted in formula-type programming mediocrity. In contrast, paid cable stations such as HBO and Showtime or new content-originators such as Netflix, designed for target customer pleasure rather than ratings and advertising, have offered innovative shows like the Sopranos, Homeland, and House of Cards that would not have been conceivable on commercial television.

One approach to change how we think about the challenge of subjectivity is to look for experience gaps.[3] Here are three approaches to experience gap analysis:

- **There is a customer knowledge gap.** In this case, the provider does not have adequate knowledge of the customer's needs (especially their emotional needs), to be able to design a service that the customer will prefer. The provider may not have adequate data collection tools in place, or may not have the right behavioral and sentiment analysis skills.
- **There is a delivery gap.** The service design is inadequate to co-create the desired experience. For example, if the customer's input indicates that they desire a delivery in 24 hours, but

the provider's delivery service process has been optimized for a 48-hour order-to-delivery time, then the design is inadequate to deliver the experience. Sometimes, the front-line service delivery employee is inadequately trained or under-empowered to deliver the service the customer expects. In both cases, there is a functional design gap.

- **There is a perception gap—the provider has misunderstood the customer's emotional needs.** The service design may be functionally adequate to create the experience as the provider understands it, but the customer perceives it in a different, idiosyncratic and subjective way, and grades the experience as poor.

The emotional gap or the perception gap is often more prevalent than the functional design gap. Ironically, most businesses focus on the functional gap, because it is easier to measure.

The enterprise can be transformed with breakthrough consequences through understanding gaps in all three dimensions. To take advantage of this new insight, the organization must build new skills sets and evaluative measures for its employees.

Experience Co-Creation's New Skills

An enterprise can choose its employees and can train them to meet standards, behave in specified ways, and deploy specific skills in their work. Key performance indicators (KPIs) can be designed to measure their performance. These tenets have been the focus of Human Resources (HR) for as long as that function has been recognized.

However, the enterprise cannot choose or train its co-producers of value, its customers, in the same way. The interaction of the trained provider and the untrained customer creates new management challenges.

Consider this example. One of the authors is a long-term, loyal Hertz customer, and an experienced user of the Hertz self-service web-based reservations system. On a recent business trip, I booked a Hertz rental car in the usual way, and was reserved a Hertz rental car model I prefer using the privileged Hertz Gold user system. So far the Hertz standard system was working for me as it does for millions to provide a predictable customer experience.

I picked up the car and checked out of the airport parking lot. As I reached freeway speed on the interstate, an unsettling noise began to emanate from the left front-fender. After a few miles, a piece of plastic detached itself and spilled onto the roadway. After a few more miles, another piece fell off. With a lot of trepidation, I kept on driving. I reached my destination, feeling very unhappy. I called Hertz and reached a well-trained, experienced Hertz employee; I reported the experience and requested that Hertz bring a replacement car and pick up the disabled car. The employee, sitting in front of a computer screen with his service options displayed, explained that he is not empowered to fulfill that request. He can send a tow truck and remove the damaged vehicle, but the customer must take a cab back to the airport where he originated his rental and rent a replacement.

As a frequent business traveler, I am conditioned to expect high levels of service and awards with global airlines, global hotel chains, and credit card companies. I have experienced extraordinary service from an airline that picked me up in a 4WD vehicle, when I was stranded in a snowstorm, and drove me to an international flight on time. When I lost my credit card in the midst of a multi-stop, multi-country trip, the credit card company sent a motorcycle rider to deliver a replacement. My expectations have been raised by these experiences and I subjectively expected more from Hertz. As a result, I decided to stop using Hertz, concluding that other car rental companies are just as good (or bad).

This event illuminates multiple errors. Hertz's standards went unenforced when a faulty vehicle was allowed into service. That's an error of *execution*. Hertz's service levels were below the expectations of the customer. That's an error of *service design*. And the Hertz employee's skills were inadequate for the co-creation exchange with the customer at a time of distress. That's *a perception gap* and *emotional gap* between the customer's expectations and the provider's delivery capability that might be impossible (or unaffordable) to bridge.

Service providers must consider what kinds of execution, design, and interaction capabilities and skills are required to avoid these errors. Dealing with subjectivity is extremely hard to standardize, and it is extremely hard to customize service design that will span the entire range of customer perception variability. However, enterprises committed to the customer value co-creation will change to win with improvements to bridge the service design, perception, and emotional gap of the ongoing relationship with their customers.

Consider design as being about desire to engage in a relationship. Imagine design thinking being rooted in a deep empathy with real users. When design clicks, it brings democratic access for real benefit and the "magic happens". To contrast the Hertz negative example of service design, look at Workday, which is a cloud-based solutions software for HR and Finance that is designed with empathy as a first principle.[4]

In the co-creation of value with the customers, traditional service organization design faces two challenges.

First, a new role must be designed for the front-line employees, those who deliver and negotiate services directly with the customers at the point of consumption. In the traditional, hierarchical organization design, control is exercised via command-and-control mechanisms that define jobs via a tight set of rules and ensure that front-line employees follow those rules.

In an environment of co-creation, tight control and rigid rules are counter-productive. Each co-creation occasion with every customer has the potential to be different from every other occasion; each one is unique. The customer might be in a good mood or a bad one; be knowledgeable and reasonable about the content of the service or ignorant and unreasonable; feeling expansive about service add-ons, or feeling stingy; standing in a long line or a short one. The variables are virtually unlimited. Command-and-control cannot be effective and cannot easily contribute to co-creation of value.

Instead, front-line employees are the core providers of value production for a service company. Service excellence elevates the importance of the individual. Amidst the swirling variables and subjectivities of the interaction with the customer, front-line employees must exercise initiative, creativity, and rapid responsiveness. They must be able to assess the idiosyncratic needs of the customer and craft a tailored service solution. Ideally, they will execute with a style and in a memorable way that encourages repeat visits and the customer loyalty.

Command-and-control cannot produce this result. The organizational structure for co-creation of value is the network. Networks are knowledge-sharing structures in which individuals are nodes that can be connected in multiple ways to the knowledge that is the source of the enterprise's capabilities. The knowledge takes the form of knowledge content and processes, and can be embodied in technology and infrastructure, and expressed via training and internal communications. The front-line employee is at the edge of the network, interacting with the customer, applying the knowledge in the interaction, and feeding back to the center the new knowledge created on each such occasion. The network is empowering and supportive, but not controlling.

The second area of organizational structure change is created via self-service technologies. These technologies change the balance of inputs between the service provider and the customer for some co-creation occasions, giving the customer the opportunity to self-serve and co-create value with additional convenience, speed, and access. A simple example is the banking app on a smartphone. It replaces a service interaction with a front-line employee (bank teller) or ATM by enabling the customer to self-serve at any time and in any location for a specific, limited range of bank service transactions. In a sense, the new front-line employee in this instance is the programmer or software engineer who writes the code that enables the service transaction via the software interface. The software engineer must think like a service provider, understanding that the task is to design and deliver an experience, and not simply to write functional lines of code.

The same organizational design directives apply to the software engineer as to the front-line employee who actually delivers service. The engineer must absorb the knowledge belonging to the enterprise regarding the experience its customers seek and must deeply understand the value proposition of the enterprise to deliver this experience. Software design can no longer be simply feature and function-centric. It must be customer-centric, capable of co-creating value with that customer, and of producing software that delivers a superior experience. Software engineers are no longer solely technical experts. They must also be subject matter experts in the area of service design and delivery, and therefore in the area of understanding the customer needs and the subjective elements of the ideal service experience. By connecting to the knowledge-sharing network of the enterprise that's designed for service, they can become a T-shaped contributor: deep and specialized in software design, broad in their understanding of all the other fields that are part of the service-delivery collaboration.

In the same way, marketing and sales professionals must understand business engineering and the capabilities of software to be able to deliver end-to-end solutions for customers. Indeed, one of the great organizational challenges of the 21st century is the co-development of marketing and IT functions for truly enhancing the customer experience. We profiled this trend in our book *Improve Your Marketing to Grow Your Business* with the case example of Hyatt Regency and how its reservation system integrated marketing and IT functions.[5]

Open Internal/External Orchestration Is the New Route to Innovation

Service innovation must be continuous. In co-creation, the customer is always looking for a better service experience and searching for higher levels of service value (co-elevation). Customers compare service experiences across different providers and a range of service channels and types, eagerly seeking new routes to better outcomes. With so many sources for new ideas and initiatives, the pace of innovation is accelerated.

In this framework, the process of innovation changes from a specialized internal prescribed process-based competency of the enterprise to an internal/external orchestration of co-creation of value with the customer. Some of the business literature has defined this transition as one from a closed system of innovation to an open system.[6] The old system for innovation was to analyze external market data and process it internally into new concepts that could be tested for market-place acceptance. The new, service-dominant system is to continuously test current offerings for customer acceptance and to utilize customer dissatisfaction or unfavorable comparisons or unmet service needs in the co-creation of service improvements. The interaction and the knowledge flow are unbroken. Innovation is not an occasional market event or even a series of step-ups in performance. Rather, it is a continuous and uninterrupted process, a way of doing business, inseparable from everyday operations.

One way to capture the essence of the new route to innovation is via crowdsourcing. In this innovation methodology, innovation tasks are assigned to a large, public group of people external to the enterprise. In some cases, this approach has been formalized. Kaggle is a digital service where programmers can get paid for creating the best programs for a given problem. The Allstate Corp turned to Kaggle when it was seeking a better algorithm to help it assess automobile insurance risks. In the 2013 Super Bowl TV broadcast, Doritos brand from Pepsico featured ads that were crowdsourced from their customers in a competition. Entrepreneur Peter Diamandis (creator of the X-prize Foundation for fostering technology competitions) has expressed the belief that crowdsourcing could entirely displace the internal innovation processes of large, vertically integrated businesses.[7]

Customer Sentiment and Behavior Data Open the Door to Loyalty

Two new data streams emerge as important in the world of co-creation of value: customer sentiment data and customer behavior data.

These two data streams provide the new underpinnings for an established foundational equation in marketing: in order to change behavior, marketers must first change sentiment. The behavior we seek is to get the customers to buy our service, to stay loyal, and to advocate it to others. The sentiment that precedes this behavior is their attitude to our service: they may ignore it, they may be biased against it, or they may be open to it; but, in the absence of a strong endorsement or other incentive, they have no reason to change their current behavior.

This elevates customer sentiment to a new level of importance. The path to customer loyalty and to service franchise value can be depicted as a continuous loop of interaction as seen in Figure 2.1.

The first phase of the loop occurs before purchase and before the service experience. In this phase, the customer may be seeking a solution to an existing need and is in planning and information-gathering mode. He or she might search blogs, visit Yelp or a similar customer-rating app, search the Internet, and visit the websites of the providers and commentators. The customer may be looking for pointers and reassurance on the fit of potential services with their personal needs or their business needs,

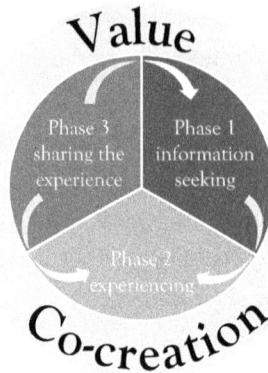

Figure 2.1. Value co-creation.

matching their logistics needs, meeting their pricing criteria, or a combi-nation of all these attributes and more. This information-gathering phase brings the customer into contact not only with facts, but also with the sentiment in the marketplace about the provider. The quality of that sen-timent will play a role in whether or not the customer advances to Phase 2 on the path to loyalty.

The second phase is the actual encounter with the service. The cus-tomer tries, buys, and utilizes the service. The output is not a transaction but an experience, measured both against the provider's promise of what the experience *will* be and the customer's own perception of what the experience *should* be. If the experience matches both those benchmarks, it will be evaluated positively and create positive sentiment. If it falls short, it will generate negative sentiment. That sentiment, positive or negative or mixed, permanently enters the information sphere as word of mouth, ratings, e-mail messages, blog entries, social media commentary, and many other forms of digital communication.

The third phase is the sharing of the experience. This element of co-creation is a new product of the social economy. Customers actively project reports and commentary about their experience into their social network. They are, in fact, providing a service of their own in the form of knowledge-sharing that can assist others in making a good service selection decision. Potential customers actively consume this knowledge, seeking it out, weighing the value of different opinions, attributing varying values to recency, frequency, and the source of the data: someone I may know; someone I may respect; someone who may merit an opinion. They enter into social conversations to dig deeper into the sentiment stream in order to formulate a more informed opinion and knowledge-based selection.

Two streams of data are produced on the path to loyalty. One is the behavioral stream. The behavioral stream can include click stream data during Phase 1 as the customer searches for information, and application data, transaction data, and payment data, as well as geo-location data (where did the customer use the service, for example), in Phase 2. These data can aggregate into databases from which to make analytical predictions (for example, which applicants for homeowner insurance are most likely to make claims, based on projections from the known behavior and known attributes of existing policy owners?).

The second stream is the sentiment stream. Analytics are now capable of identifying sentiment trends and sentiment substance from unstructured data like e-mails and blogs and social media. The linking of sentiment and behavior becomes more of a quantifiable relationship and makes the business of marketing more of a data-based science than an artistry without predictability.

The Impact on Marketing

Marketing is entering a new era as a consequence of the rise of Service Thinking. We will explore some of the changes to this most important of business disciplines in subsequent chapters. Here, we can summarize the new way of marketing with the help of a simple FROM-TO chart.

FROM	TO
Target individuals or segments by behavior, attitude or demographics.	Broad view of the service system context in which customers pursue their goals.
Find insights into causality of behavior based on their needs and motivations.	Understand social interactions and emerging social sentiment.
Make a unique promise about brand benefits.	Fit in rather than assert.
Deliver on the claims in the promise via superior features and attributes.	Make a propositon to contribute to the service system and the social culture.
Actively develop and attractive character for the brand to bond with the target customer.	Provide transparency (including how the brand interacts with non-customers)
Didactic	Dialectic

Figure 2.2. Marketing in the era of Service Thinking.

In the left-hand column, we can summarize traditional marketing through its concepts of targeting customers, seeking to understand the causes of customer behavior, making a brand promise based on a claim of superior features and attributes compared to the customer's current brand, and massaging perceptions through the concept of brand character, or a desirable brand "personality."

In the right-hand column, we depict marketing in the Service Thinking era as taking a much more humble approach. The discipline should seek to understand the customer's context and service system, and the social interactions and sentiments in which the customer is involved. Marketing's task is to seek permission to enter this service system by demonstrating—if invited—an ability to fit in and make a contribution. Fitting in demands transparency not just in the service interaction with the customer but in the relationship of the brand to the customer's entire service system and social culture. That's why social and environmental responsibility takes on new importance in branded offerings.

Brands must become more humble ("How can we be of service today?") and less iconic ("The ultimate driving machine").

Co-Creation Changes Everything

The principle that all value is co-created and that value is realized in an experience, which is determined by the subjective perception of the customer, is the fundamental driver of the Service Thinking approach. Once businesses have absorbed and embraced this principle, they can move on to consideration of the systemic consequences. We explore those implications in Chapter 3.

CHAPTER 3

Service Systems: Specialization Plus Integration

Always design a thing by considering it in its next largest context—a chair in a room, a room in a house, a house in an environment, an environment in a city plan.

—Frank Lloyd Wright

To illustrate the transformational impact of Service Thinking on business, we now expand our analysis from one-to-one service design and delivery to service systems. Service systems are the new form of business architecture.

While the service interaction is often between two individuals—such as the hotel guest checking in with the front desk attendant or the bank customer dealing with the teller—the service delivery is always between two "service systems." Service systems are a combination of multiple components and connections—an assembly of people, knowledge, and technology offering a value proposition.

Consider an enterprise such as a major retailer or a hardware manufacturer seeking to launch an integrated communications campaign. The company does not design, produce, or distribute communications itself; it engages one or more third parties (such as an advertising agency, a media buying company, and a social media company) to do so.

Before a request for proposal can be published to any of these third parties, however, there is an internal service system that enables the action. The brand manager may be the initiator of the request, and the integrator of the system, with authorization from the Vice President of Marketing. The marketing planning process may have established the need for the advertising and communications, and ROI analysis of historical advertising expenditures may have been conducted to justify the expenditure. Finance must be involved to confirm that the expenditure can be

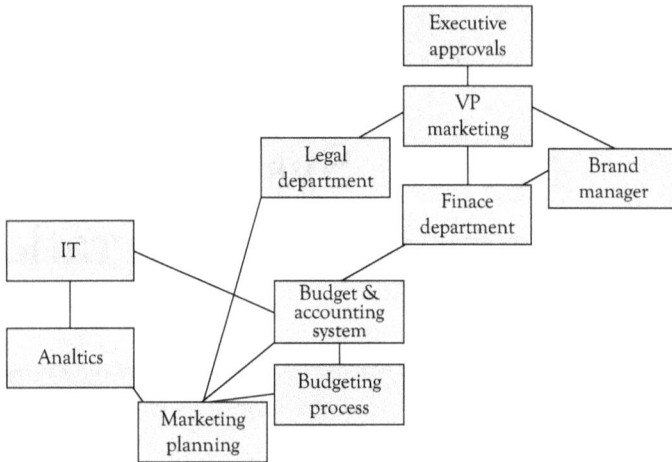

Figure 3.1. Customer service system for an advertising campaign (Illustrative).

undertaken. The legal department will be alerted to help ensure that any claims or statements made in communications have legal approval. The executive wing will be involved both for authorizations and approvals. Perhaps the sales department is engaged in advance of the campaign to plan appropriately for additional sales.

Once the internal service system is aligned and activated, the brand manager can make a connection to one or more outside vendors who specialize in communication services. Let's assume that a marketing agency has already been appointed to respond to service requests such as this one. (The term in the industry is "agency of record"—a recognition of a durable connection between the enterprise and its specialist service supplier for repetitive services. Such durable connections have benefits in faster and clearer information exchanges between the two service systems and accelerated mutual adaptation to facilitate superior service outcomes.)

The marketing agency will assemble a service system for the task that comprises both internal specialist competencies and external competencies. Internally, the account director may be the first line of contact with the client brand manager. The account director will get authorization from his or her head of department and the agency's financial department to activate the agency's resources to respond to the RFP. Those resources will include multiple departments and specialized knowledge, skills, and

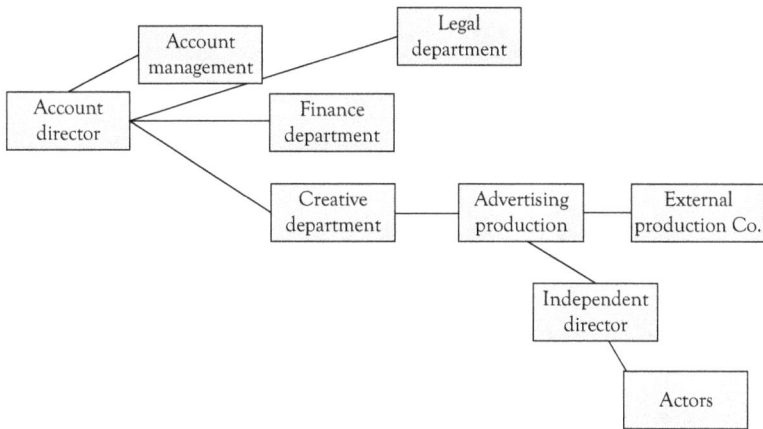

Figure 3.2. Provider service system for an advertising campaign (Illustrative).

abilities: the creative department specializing in persuasive words and images, the production department specializing in bringing the creative to visual or printed form, the legal department that will both parse the legal risk for the agency and advise the client, the finance department to estimate and approve costs, and senior management for internal co-ordination and executive approvals.

The internal agency specialist will implement some of these specialized functions by reaching out to external super-specialists. For video, an agency production manager typically will engage an independent video director and an independent video production company to find a site to shoot the video, facilitate casting and hiring, assemble all the equipment, deliver it to the set, and even cater the event. Actors and actresses are typically independent contractors. If the video is animated, a specialized animation company will be hired.

The video communication is an example of a service system assembled for a specialized service delivery task—the production of the video—and then immediately disassembled so that the component elements can be reassembled for another customer in the future.

The internal service system at the customer and the external service system of the marketing agency co-create the service of producing a commercial video. The service systems will then be re-ordered for the next stage of service. A media planning company will be connected to the

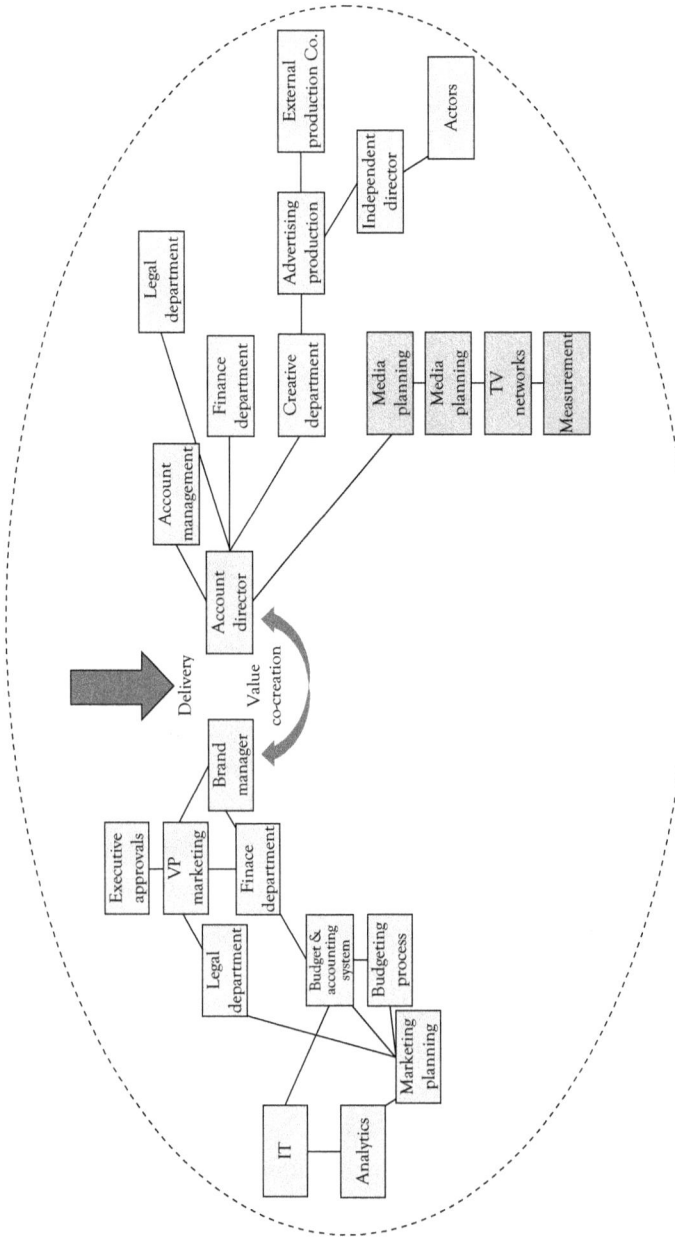

Figure 3.3. Provider–Customer service systems integrated for value co-creation.

service system to advise on where the video should be shown and the price of purchasing that distribution service. Then the traditional distribution networks like NBC, ABC, CBS, and Fox, and Cable Networks such as ESPN, will be engaged, as well as local media stations; Google AdWords and other Internet-based communications platforms may be added as well. A measurement company will be engaged to measure the number of people watching when the video is shown. An analytics company will be brought in, to ascertain the increase in sales revenues, brand image perception, and engagement (Net Promoter Score, both behavior and sentiment analysis, etc.) as a result of the communication campaign. This is a new phase of co-creation of value—the analysis of the experience and behavior of the ultimate customer in order to guide future resource allocation.

Specialization and Integration

This illustration of the interaction between and within two service systems that combine to co-create value is one of a countless number of such service systems in the global economy. Service systems are everywhere; understanding them is an important component of the co-creation of value.

Service systems have a profound impact on business architecture. We defined the service system as an assembly of people, knowledge, and technology with a value proposition. The customer is the assembler of the service system and will continually refine the system in the search for the best outcome, defined as the best service experience and most efficient and effective delivery of the service. For each component of the service system, the customer will aim to identify the highest form of specialized knowledge for that component, the most developed and proven skills and abilities, the best support and delivery technologies, and the people who can design and deliver the best service experience, all consistent with low cost, fast speed, and flexibility. Co-elevation is a continuous improvement characteristic of good service systems. Because the customer service system demands and seeks better and better service via specialization, the provider service system is required to continually improve by improving knowledge, technology, and the capability of its people to deliver service.

Consider how the de-regulation of airline pricing has unleashed two service systems to co-create new value through co-elevation. Airlines, operating sophisticated online pricing tools, can now change prices daily per flight to reflect the customized value of every seat to every passenger. Customers can hire online intermediaries such as Kayak, Expedia, and Priceline to navigate the new airline pricing offerings and generate a range of choices, replacing traditional travel agents. The two co-evolved service systems of providers and customers have created a far more efficient market, lowering airfares for customers and increasing the passenger yield per flight for providers.[1]

A provider company must have developed a unique specialization for the customer's assembled service system to give it a competitive advantage in that area of competency and therefore qualify it for inclusion. Additionally, it must prove capable of performing as part of the larger service system, with smooth information exchanges, and frictionless interaction with other components for the benefit of the customer. The value proposition is that, for this particular component of the service system, the supplier company is the best choice for the delivery of the desired service experience, and for working with all other components for effective and efficient outcomes.

This is "*specialization plus integration,*" necessary for designing the successful enterprise of the future. The successful service provider company will continually reinforce its specialist competencies, while ensuring that every element required for integration with other service system components is sufficiently well-developed, coherent (all important processes are included), and flawless in implementation.

The specialized and integrated enterprise of the future can take many forms to fit into the relevant service system. The enterprise may be very small because it has an acute specialization—for example, a developer of apps for the iPhone. The same enterprise must be highly integrated (into the iPhone service system) to ensure continued relevance and business flow. Alternatively, the enterprise may be large because its specialization is wide. For example, Smithfield Foods specializes in bringing fresh and processed pork products to the tables of consumers the world over. It is highly integrated both backwards into the supply chain of farmers and growers, and forward into distribution service systems and retail service systems. Potentially, an enterprise can be enormous and globe-spanning like IBM or WalMart. These companies will become modular assemblies of internal specializations linked together for the benefit of customers and other stakeholders, as well as externally linked to additional specializations that they can assemble and deploy for their customers.

We will look deeper into the tools and trends in modular business architecture in the next chapter. However, first let's consider some of the change implications of service systems.

The Role of Strategy

Business strategy has become a systematized discipline. Conventional practices prescribe a proactive process, based on a situation analysis of trends, internal strengths and weaknesses, and external forces to develop calculations of enterprise-level competitive advantage. Presumably, well-conceived and implemented strategic planning is measured by revenue growth, high market share, profitability, share price appreciation—that is, financial metrics, competitively benchmarked against industry competitors, and financial market norms. An over-arching, top-down strategy, based on market assumptions, should win.

Strategy has a humbler role in Service Thinking. The goal is to fit in to one or more service systems and to contribute to desirable outcomes for customers. Specialization and integration are forces that compel the examination of competencies that will tend to narrow and intensify the enterprise focus rather than expand it. Each specialization must be examined to ascertain whether or not the enterprise can be the best at it, that is, create absolute advantage. If not, it is better to let another, superior specialist perform that role and to externally integrate with that specialist in a value web within a shared service system.

Because specialization and integration in service systems are continuously evolving, strategy becomes an *emergent* feature of the business rather than a prescriptive planning tool. The enterprise is constantly exploring its options for specialization and its best connections to external specialists to assemble the most effective and efficient service system. In this swirling, ever-changing environment of new specialties and new connections, the top-down strategy hinders rather than enables. Continuous adaptation to evolving service systems will require at minimum a new set of conditional, accommodative strategy tools, and quite possibly the ditching of the entire concept of business strategy. The replacement will be a network view—connection and integration of shared value co-creation networks, continuously changing and evolving under the principle of specialization and integration.

Marketing and Brand Building

Peter Drucker, who is considered the founder of management science, stated that there are only two major results-generating functions of the business enterprise: innovation and marketing.[2] In Chapter 2, we discussed the impact of Service Science Thinking and Co-Creation on the process of innovation. We also began to consider the requisite changes in marketing in the context of co-creation of value. The concept of service systems further impacts and changes the fundamentals of marketing.

Business has been very focused on brand building, which has been viewed as the core function of marketing. Brands have been viewed as intellectual property assets that can generate long-term cash flows from customer brand loyalty, generating higher prices and margins based on those customers' preferences. Brand building tools have been assertive and didactic. Brand owners seek to build iconic brands, establish performance superiority, and claim authenticity, with the goal of brand dominance. Brands make promises and assert their uniqueness. Brands demand attention and notice, always seeking to "break through." Brands offer solutions.

In Service Thinking, this view becomes modified. While brand recognition and identity have their place, the new brand emphasis is on fitting in (consonance) and contributing (resonance) to the customer's service system. Moreover, the brand itself is part of a service system, never a stand-alone entity. Fitting in elevates the customer's search for service system coherence above aspirations to meet individual needs with individual brands and solutions. (For example, if a customer is planning an all-inclusive vacation through Expedia to Hawaii, the airline brand may matter less than the convenience of the flight schedule and whether the airline is a component in the package.) When viewed through the lens of service branding, the traditional hierarchy of needs is replaced with a shared value network map. The customer is continually adding nodes, strengthening important points of convergence, optimizing information sharing routes, filtering in information that strengthens their service system cohesion and filtering out components and information that do the opposite, and elevating or reducing the importance of some service system features and inhabitants. Brands that fit in well and make contributions to the customer's service system are allocated increased importance and lasting roles. If they don't contribute, they are by-passed and excluded from the network.

The implications of this service science view of branding are significant:

1. Brands should no longer be engineered to "stand for one thing" or "own a benefit." These standard marketing aphorisms refer to a product-dominant world, not a service-dominant world. Brands now need to adapt themselves to a variety of social and service system networks and trends in order to fit in. Logos, packaging, messages, design elements, tactics, and innovations will all be flexible. The brand might be different on different days or in different countries or for different service system networks.

2. Brands will not manage their relationships with the customers; they will fit in to customers' systems. There is a meaningful difference in behavior and attitude between the two roles. Fitting in is more humble. Fitting in is not just listening, but learning. When customers co-create, brands must sometimes adopt a deferential role. When Instagram updated its terms of service but neglected to be clear about the changes that would be made to the social network, its users immediately voiced concern, including power user National Geographic. Instagram quickly responded to the outrage and reversed its decision to update the terms of service.[3] Coca-Cola's switch from ICONIC ("It's the real thing") to CONSONANT ("happiness") is a similar example of the humbler approach.

3. Brand concepts like "authenticity", "icon", "status", and "solution" no longer apply. They are assertions about what the brand can do for the customer. In the services world, the customer controls the role

that the brand plays, and decides on that role on the basis of how the brand fits into their service system network.

4. Brand research will migrate from asking questions to observing behavior and listening to service systems using social tools.

5. Brand execution will be dynamically responsive to the data that emerges from observing behavior and listening to the networks. Annual plans and spending allocations will be replaced by flexible response mechanisms.

Organizational Design

Design thinking focuses on the performance of a system in order to design the role of component parts of the system. Service Thinking requires the examination of collaborative and adaptive capabilities and information flows. And it implies the use of learning to continuously improve system attributes.

However, the constraints of traditional organizational design have hindered the potential for innovative design thinking to co-create value. Sometimes this is because of the legacy effect—organizations pre-exist; the new design and change management from old to new is daunting. Another influence is the power of hierarchy and silos. Try as they might, most company management teams have failed in the effort to dump the organization chart and silos such as "strategic business units."

To thrive in the world of service systems, organizational design must find a way to throw off the legacy shackles. We must question the entire concept of organizational boundaries, both internal and external, and consider replacement with internal and external integration. When the front-line employee is the one who delivers service and is responsible for the customer's service experience, we must rethink hierarchy and the relationship between front-line and management. When strategy becomes emergent rather than prescriptive, we must re-think the role of the executive suite.

The route to a new science of organizational design follows the path of modular business architecture. To explain this, we will examine Component Business Architecture in Chapter 4.

CHAPTER 4

Designing Organizations for Specialization and Integration: Modular Business Architecture

If we have 17 million customers, we should have 17 million stores.[1]
—Jeff Bezos (CEO, Amazon)

Service systems are highly dynamic. The providers, driving to improve their value proposition and offer the best possible experience to the customers, are constantly seeking to upgrade and will substitute one vendor for another if there is the possibility of a service improvement. The customers, similarly driven to seek a better service experience, will switch from one provider to another if there is a service improvement.

At the same time, service systems are becoming more open to competition. Global communications networks, cloud computing, and open technology standards make it possible for any enterprise to compete efficiently in any industry. CRM platforms and social business tools enable responsiveness for all firms. Cloud analytics can make deep insights available to all who seek them and can fuel rapid innovation throughout an industry. This portends radical change for business architecture and the emergence of new vendors to industries who can offer new specialized benefits.

Control Strategy Is Obsolete

Enterprises must now focus on establishing absolute advantage in their industry domains to leverage these dynamic technological advances. Inertia and defense of the status quo will result in loss of market position. In the past, the enterprise may have pursued a strategy of control to maintain market position, for example, controlling industry value chains, either by designing for end-to-end capabilities, or by partnering with other enterprises to establish shared control. The Japanese system of keiretsu in the 20th Century was a good example of a shared control system.

Similarly, enterprises may seek to exert internal control via strategic business units, which are essentially end-to-end internal supply chains, pursuing an internal organizational strategy that reflects the goal of external market control.

Such market control is a mirage. The Service Thinking enterprise can only maintain its place in the service system by providing the best service with an *absolute advantage*. The advantage is based on both internal KPIs and the customer perceptions. The drive for absolute advantage spurs a new organizational design trend: componentization. Componentized Business Architecture is the appropriate response to the *specialization* and *integration* of service systems:

Specialization—becoming the best by focusing narrowly on a specific set of specialized knowledge and directing investment single-mindedly to the further development of that specialized knowledge.

Integration—assembling specialized modules (whether internal to the enterprise or external to it) into a service system of unparalleled excellence, capable of delivering service in the smoothest, most seamless way possible. The modern enterprise must define and assemble business modules that are the absolute best at the specialized set of activities that they perform. These modules must have the right resources (people, processes, and technologies), superior skills, and knowledge, and the appropriate capital assets operating at the most efficient level, and the right informatics to continuously refine that efficiency level. The large-scale enterprise is a federation of these self-governing business modules.

Componentized Business Architecture

The design tool for this modular business organization is Componentized Business Architecture. Components are the building blocks of the new globally integrated enterprise. They have five characteristics:

- They have a distinct business purpose, a reason to exist within the enterprise, specifically for the benefit of the value proposition to the customer.
- They house a mutually exclusive set of business activities, not reproduced anywhere else in the enterprise.
- They have the required resources to perform these activities: tangible and intangible assets (including specialized knowledge), people and technologies, and skills. Taken together and applied for the business purpose, we may call this bundle of resources a capability.
- They constitute an independent entity with its own governance model and processes; theoretically, each could operate independently.
- They provide and receive services from other internal or external modules in an integrated service system, using service level agreements to define the quality of service exchange.

Each component is highly cohesive; it houses similar people, skills, processes, and technologies, performing only activities that belong there and are reproduced nowhere else in the enterprise. Each component has its own distinctive set of KPIs to measure performance. Successful specialized enterprises build these components once and then deploy them across many channels and interfaces. For example, a bank may build a credit decision-making component and apply it to consumer loans and business loans, mortgages and credit lines, small business customers, and large business customers. Professional credit specialists in the component will use a set of tools developed for their purpose and share knowledge and data to continuously improve loan productivity and performance. As they do so, they develop the kind of absolute advantage in credit decision-making processes to support specialization.

Similarly, a retailer may build a customer service component and deploy it for online sales and in-store sales, ensuring that the customer enjoys a consistent experience irrespective of whether the interface is online or offline, or in the store. This specialization in customer service may prevent disruption of the retailer's business model by online-only entrants.

Componentized Business Architecture is a framework to design the federation of business modules for the enterprise and to map out organizational advancement toward optimum specialization and integration. The framework has two dimensions: competencies and control levels. A generic version is illustrated in Figure 4.1

The horizontal dimension arrays the competencies of the enterprise. Different firms will map their competencies in different ways, but the groupings must (a) contain all the activities the firm undertakes and (b) include all the capabilities required to compete in the identified field of business. In this illustration, we've defined competencies as Manage, Design, Buy, Make, and Sell.

On the vertical axis are the resources of the enterprise, applied in business activities via the appropriate control mechanisms. They are grouped into four types: Providing direction (vision and strategy); learning (knowledge management, R&D, innovation); exerting control (oversight and management); and implementing (production and maintenance).

Each of these control levels requires different collections of resources: different people with different knowledge and skills; different processes acting on different types of data; different technologies; and sometimes, different physical resources.

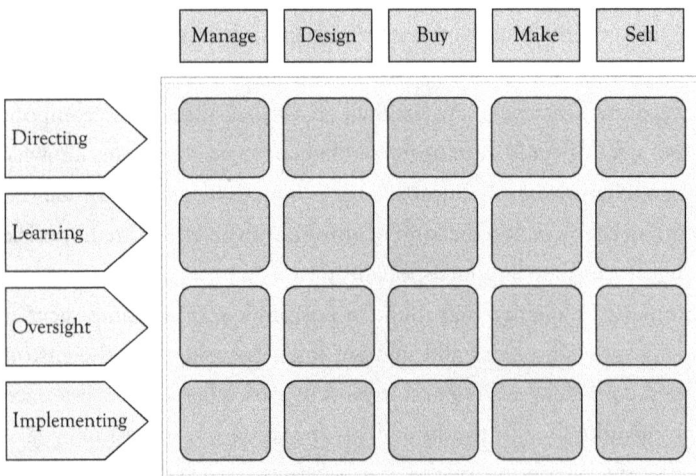

Figure 4.1. Building blocks of the component business model.

Business components lie at the intersection of the competencies and resources. They combine the activities of the firm and the resources utilized in those activities.

For example, a retailer must have competencies in

- customer management—segmentation, targeting, marketing and communications, and customer service;
- products—planning, design, development, procurement, supply chain management, inventory, and replenishment;
- channels—channel strategy, store design (online and offline), staffing and labor, construction, security, and real estate;
- logistics—supply network, warehousing, demand planning, routing, transportation, and delivery;
- business administration—corporate strategy, planning and governance, performance management and analytics, treasury, risk management, legal and regulatory, accounting and reporting, and IT systems and operations.

The competencies array can be performed at the industry, firm or line-of-business, or even function level as a disciplined analysis of areas of capability required to compete and potential sources of advantage.

Create Your Own Componentized Architecture

Using this analysis framework, any enterprise can develop its own advantaged, scalable and adaptable organization, and continuously refine it and improve it:

1. Map the competencies and resources of the enterprise in a Componentized Architecture framework as described above. We've shown the example of the retailer in the model form in Figure 4.2.
2. Based on the insights from the customer trend analysis, competitive analysis, and enterprise analytics, one can identify hot spots on the component business model grid that represent strategic opportunities. These are typically in four areas: opportunities for differentiation, opportunities for revenue growth, opportunities for margin expansion, and opportunities for cost reduction/capital optimization.

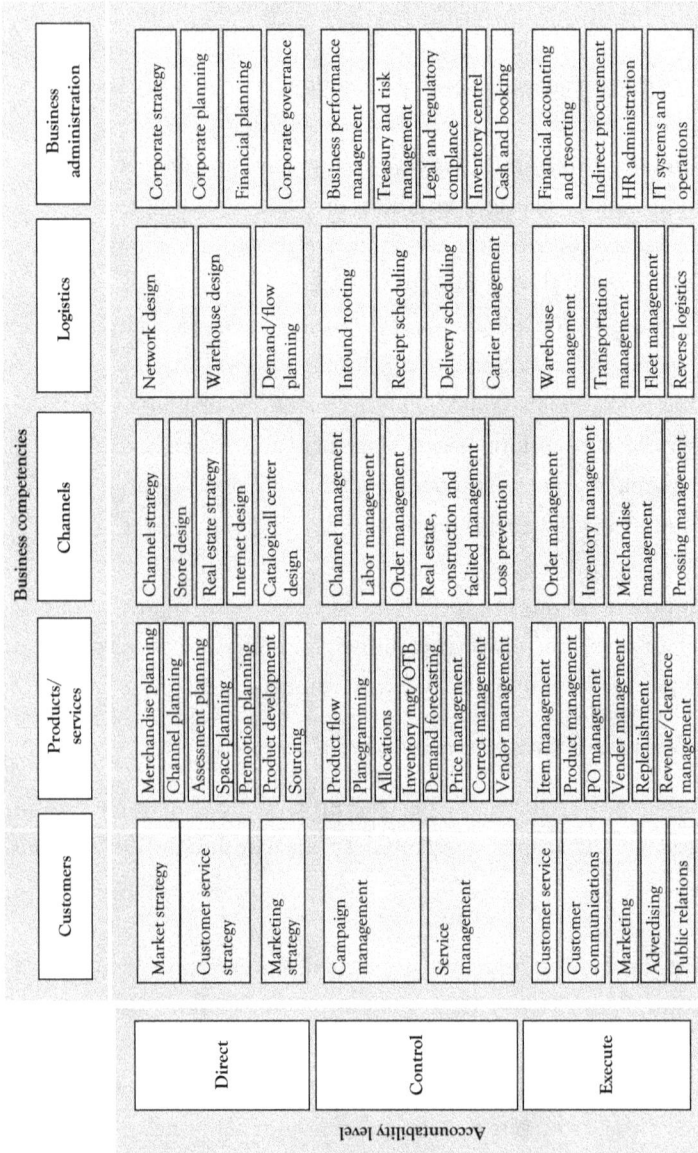

Business competencies

Accountability level

	Customers	Products/services	Channels	Logistics	Business administration
Direct	Market strategy; Customer service strategy; Marketing strategy	Merchandise planning; Channel planning; Assessment planning; Space planning; Premotion planning; Product development; Sourcing	Channel strategy; Store design; Real estate strategy; Internet design; Catalogicall center design	Network design; Warehouse design; Demand/flow planning	Corporate strategy; Corporate planning; Financial planning; Corporate goverance
Control	Campaign management; Service management	Product flow; Planegramming; Allocations; Inventory mgt/OTB; Demand forecasting; Price management; Correct management; Vendor management	Channel management; Labor management; Order management; Real estate, construction and faclited management; Loss prevention	Intound rooting; Receipt scheduling; Delivery scheduling; Carrier management	Business performance management; Treasury and risk management; Legal and regulatory compliance; Inventory centrel; Cash and booking
Execute	Customer service; Customer communications; Marketing; Adverdising; Public relations	Item management; Product management; PO management; Vender management; Replenishment; Revenue/clearence management	Order management; Inventory management; Merchandise management; Prossing management	Warehouse management; Transportation management; Fleet management; Reverse logistics	Financial accounting and resorting; Indirect procurement; HR administration; IT systems and operations

Figure 4.2. Mapping the enterprise as a network of business modules: an example from the retail industry.
Source: IBM Business Consulting Services.

3. Identify those components where the enterprise has gaps or redundancies to resolve. Gaps are missing resources, competitively underperforming activities (i.e., lacking absolute advantage), or incompletely developed capabilities. Redundancies are activities that are performed in more than one component or are better performed by an external firm than by yours.

4. For each of the gaps and resources, make a specialization choice.

   a. **Is this a component** for which we should seek internal specialization for the absolute advantage. If so, what are the resources to be acquired or developed, what is the investment level, and what are the returns?

   b. **Is this a component** for which we should seek external specialization, and integrate the absolute advantage of a specialist partner into our offering?

5. Architect the future enterprise as if these choices have been made and executed.

Draw a roadmap to get from where you are today to the architecture of the future, with appropriate investment levels and returns analysis.

KPIs and Metrics

Once you have conceived a Service Thinking Componentized Business Architecture, measure and track comparative performance and improvements of each business component. What are its contributions to the service system and what is its absolute advantage position and grade (degree of advantage)? Since each component is characterized by both providing and receiving services, the metrics must be service metrics—multisided to reflect the co-creation of value—and must be capable of being captured in service level agreements (SLAs) so that each component can contract to a certain level of service quality and the customer can ascertain whether or not that level of quality is consistently achieved.

The essential KPIs for each module will include

- cost, benchmarked to the most competitive cost in the industry;
- revenue (if any) generated by the module;

- adherence to service level agreement (speed, quality, and service features);
- perception of service quality and service experience by the customer (internal or external);
- use of people (number and salaries);
- use of capital;
- generation of capital and other assets (intellectual property, patents, knowledge, and tools).

In order to achieve best-in-class efficiency and effectiveness performance in each module, the enterprise must be capable of generating the KPI data, monitoring over time, and benchmarking against dynamic industry standards.

Componentization in Action

One of the results of modularizing business models using this tool has been the emergence of componentization—a new form of business architecture that combines modules from multiple enterprises in reconfigurable *value webs* that fuel new levels of value co-creation. *Value webs* are formed from modules that can offer services through standardized interfaces to create new business configurations in areas such as supply chain management.[2] For example:

- FedEx and UPS provide components that help their customers offer on-demand customer service. Any company can offer FedEx and UPS delivery services to their own customers, including premium services such as tracking and overnight or Saturday delivery. There is no need for a retailer or other enterprise to create a delivery or outbound logistics component in their business model; instead the enterprise can offer it by integrating the FedEx or UPS componentized offering into its own offering. Any retailer of any size anywhere on the web or anywhere on earth can compete on logistics at world-class quality and cost by integrating these components into their business.

- Amazon provides components to enable other retailers to use Amazon's platform for e-commerce. These third-party retailers can move excess inventory, manage financial transactions, warehouse and deliver using Amazon components. A fine jeweler or a gourmet food supplier does not need to build an e-commerce, or buyer review or shipping logistics capability; they simply plug in to Amazon components to do the job.

- Li & Fung is a Hong Kong based service provider to retail chains all over the world. The company provides supply chain services to retailers by linking them (and their data) to a value web of manufacturers, assemblers, cutters, sewers, tailors, fabric makers, button makers, dyers, warehousers, truckers, shippers, and customs forwarders. The retailer communicates orders (or perhaps just inventory positions) to Li & Fung, who, in turn, activates the appropriate components in the value web to get the required product to the right retailer (sometimes direct to the store) in the right sizes at the right time. Li & Fung does not own any of the facilities used in the process, but they do provide the standardized interface to communicate and track orders, and to manage transactions and logistics. Li & Fung designs and monitors the process and the IT backbone that binds the components together.

- Walmart adopted P&G's inventory management component as a capability, and thereby transformed their supplier/retailer relationship. P&G has a componentized capability to count inventory, deliver replenishment, stock shelves, and fore-cast future sales, via its link to Walmart's point-of-sale data. There's a win-win opportunity to both parties to keep product in stock and optimize sales throughput while minimizing inventory. P&G can offer the same componentized capability to another retailer simply by plugging in to a different data stream, so long as the interface is standardized.

- Toyota is building an efficient global production platform by integrating its assembly plants so that the componentry of dif-ferent models can be plugged into a common assembly line. In different countries, components of labor or capital (robots)

can be utilized depending on costs, and a wide variety of
models tailored to local needs can be assembled, while saving
time and money. Because of the ability to fill market niches
efficiently, Toyota's componentized business model can drive
growth as well as lowering costs.

Modularized business architectures enable specialization with integration. Specialization adopts the best practice, whether that best practice is
located inside the enterprise or outside. Integration makes all the components work together via standardized interfaces and integrated platforms,
offering the customer ease-of-use, speed, and efficiency. Value webs that
operate on a network principle, not a control principle, replace vertically
integrated industries and horizontally linked supply chains. Value webs
are invitational—they invite any qualified enterprise to join if they bring
communication, co-ordination, and collaboration.

The enterprise is now an open architecture. Scale and market power
are no longer guarantees of dominance. The growth prize goes to the agile
and the connected.

CHAPTER 5

Glo-Mo-So Scalable Platforms

For technology to create the most leverage in services, it can't support only industrial solutions—it has to support services solutions.

—John Arthur Ricketts

"Does it scale?"

That's the question Nilofer Merchant, author of *11 Rules for Creating Value in the Social Era*, reports CEOs ask when she talks about the "social era" of business—her inclusive term for many of the transformative elements of Service Thinking.[1]

The question reveals the mental barriers to Service Thinking rooted in manufacturing and product-centric paradigms. Large scale became an end itself ("bigger is better"). Viewed as a rich source of competitive advantage, scale could bring efficiency via the experience curve, input cost reduction via procurement power, and market power in the form of pricing command and broad distribution. We learned that market share was the metric of success for large-scale companies, over which "titans" would battle for leadership.

As we explained in Chapter 4, Service Thinking disrupts traditional presumptions about scale through Componentized Business Architecture. Providers who assemble service systems will continuously seek to replace underperforming service system components with alternatives that deliver better performance in meeting the customer's need. This service system force will generate more and more specialization, as industry players identify ways to innovate in a component or sub-component.

Doesn't this hyper-specialization lead to the opposite of scale? Is it therefore inefficient in the long run? It is tempting for conventional businesses to think this way, because scale has always been a driver of business activities, whether via mergers and acquisitions or building bigger and more integrated manufacturing facilities (capital structure costs). But Service Thinking is different, because specialization is always accompanied by integration. The potential power of the Cloud and virtual networks change the calculus for scale and distribution in the globally integrated enterprise (GIE).

Global Connectivity Platform

Several recent technology innovations have combined to create a global connectivity platform. The platform fosters low-cost collaboration and integration by offering flexible access to enterprises, entrepreneurs, multinational corporation partners, vendors, and suppliers. Challenging and weakening traditional business structures and boundaries, this global connectivity platform replaces traditional concepts of scale.[2] Consider how Skype, as a start-up, used the Internet connectivity platform— without investing in building it—to disrupt the economic model for long distance international telephone calling.

The global connectivity platform integrates three symbiotic influences:

1. Communications networks have made digital connectivity faster and more affordable. More companies can collaborate, interoperate, and share information at higher speeds and often in real time. Whatever their size, wherever their location, whenever their time zone, all enterprises can utilize modern broadband and wireless communications technologies.

2. Foundational enterprise software technologies are now broadly available to all enterprises at affordable cost. ERP (Enterprise Resource Planning) and CRM (Customer Relationship Management) software—the fundamental software enabling the front and back end of the enterprise—can be purchased by the hour and by the user (you do not have to build the infrastructure, you can rent it and benefit from continuous upgrades). Forrester Research, in fact, cites SaaS (software as a service) and data-driven smart apps as the major growth engines for the worldwide software market.[3] Business integration software is widely available so that all kinds of enterprises can fully utilize these capabilities. Shared infrastructure and common

solutions enable firms to seek and cement partnerships and advance to new levels of collaboration and integration.

3. Third, open standards provide the final key to opening the doors of global specialization and integration to all. These open standards apply in both technology and business. On the business side, the ability to define common processes and activities enables enterprises to piece together new solutions quickly from disparate components, from both internal and external sources. On the technology side, open standards such as XML (extensible markup language) are being adopted by a majority of businesses. These are simple, gratis open standards, and usable across the Internet.

In combination, the global connectivity platform attributes lower transaction costs, resulting in decreasing barriers to entry for a new flowering of service enterprises. When the infrastructure barriers are lowered in this way, creativity is unleashed for the design of new advantaged components to fit into and contribute to a service system.

Mobile Apps Exemplify Disruptive Change

Mobile communications do not simply bring customers the same service delivered via a smaller device. They bring a qualitatively different form of service, and a co-elevation capability that improves the value of using mobile in ways that were impossible to imagine with the analog landline telephone. Therefore, mobile communications represent a disruptive change.[4] Mobile devices have given rise to a new form of software application—the app—and a new service system to create and distribute them—the app store. The result is not only a new service experience, but also one that's available through a universal communication platform reaching billions of users, and on which billions of collaborators can interact and share. Waze, the crowd-sourced traffic-mapping and navigation company, uses live feedback from its driver network to generate real-time traffic reports and adjusts its route recommendations accordingly. Simply by identifying congested areas—enabling others to avoid the congestion-mobile-enabled drivers are co-creating a better travel experience.[5]

Many service industries have been disrupted and physically transformed by mobile computing. Music is an obvious example. The iTunes virtual store has replaced many brick and mortar music stores, and almost any garage band can produce and distribute its content to unlimited customers through YouTube. Publishing is moving in the same direction, along with the payments industry, travel agencies, news, and advertising. Mobile technology creates new manifestations of services. Value chains are shortened, costs are lowered, and service is customized.

In this environment, service providers can establish a direct software linkage with their customers, involving them directly in the co-creation process. When they can co-design service content and delivery from preferred suppliers, customers will experience a much higher level of co-created value. It becomes harder for a closed, non-mobile delivery system to compete effectively against this level of value creation, regardless of the company size or name recognition.

Social Business Software Is the Organizing Technology of Service Systems

In Chapter 3, we defined a service system as an assembly of people, knowledge, and technology with a value proposition. Social business software is the organizing technology of service systems:

- Linking people together so that they can collaborate, share knowledge, and design co-create, and deliver services.
- Organizing knowledge, both formal and tacit, structured and unstructured. This knowledge can be made available by sharing, searching, curating, and tagging. It can be presented in libraries, wikis, blogs, and streams. There is increasing understanding that unstructured data is highly useful in adaptive human collaborative processes, and social business software supports these processes with the right kind of knowledge.
- Sharing and development of specialist knowledge in specialist communities, establishing projects and conducting peer-based project management. Individuals with specialist knowledge can be socially tagged and invited to contribute from their specialist angle.
- Visualizing innovation ideas in idea banks.

- Using predictive models and prediction markets operating on social business platforms for participants to create, share, and improve "what if" scenarios.

Accelerating sharing and project management messaging rapidly among participants—instantly, real time, or time shifted.

One good example of social business software to illustrate these capabilities is Quid, co-founded by Sean Gurley and Bob Goodson in 2012. Quid has built software that augments human intelligence, transforming complex global information into actionable insight. The premise is to combine human and computerized intelligence to provide better solutions for companies and governments—a great illustration of specialization and integration.[6]

Social business software is highly conducive to co-creation of value. User ergonomics are highly customizable and navigation can be suited to the user, saving time and making users more productive. Streams and feeds can keep members of the communities current with events and developments so that more people have current knowledge and can focus on advancing rather than catching up. Traditional boundaries of hierarchy become more porous, making organizations more agile and responsive.

The value proposition for the service system catalyzed by social business software is the final element binding communities. It is shared purpose that binds collaborative communities together. People who work together in a company with a strong sense of shared purpose are more motivated, loyal, and productive. Employee networks on social business software platforms are self-governing. They come together for their shared purpose, such as meeting a quality standard for the delivery of a service, and they self-reinforce through the sharing of knowledge and skills applied to the group goal.

The social business software platform can be utilized to support service systems, combining both the customer and the service provider sides. CRM software now enables customers to contribute both their needs and proposed solutions to the service provider. The provider's internal service system can collaborate on combining multiple customer expressions of the same or similar needs, testing one or more proposed solutions, and then introducing the best solution as a new service offered across the customer-facing service system (continuous innovation).

Software developer communities frequently apply this process. An individual user can log bugs and other issues on the software company's social business software and can offer "fixes" that he or she has developed. The software company can test the "fixes" and then offer them generally to all their users. In this way, the community, both provider and customers, collaborates to raise the service quality and enhance the service experience of all participants.

In consumer markets, social platforms such as Yelp enable consumers to share ratings, comments, and other observations about the service experience provided by businesses. Their peers can utilize this information to adjust their own service systems, and the providers can analyze the sentiments expressed as input to service improvement initiatives. Again, the impact is to raise the level of service quality (co-elevate) on both the provider and customer side of the service system.

Glo-Mo-So

Global-mobile-social (Glo-Mo-So) platforms enable service producers to combine three elements: integration via the global communications platform, universal delivery via mobile devices, and collaboration across service systems via social business software. When, at the same time, they also adopt the componentized business architecture recommended in Chapter 4, they become successful globally integrated enterprises.

They focus on three goals: differentiation, responsiveness, and efficiency.

Differentiation is achieved by designing business components with absolute advantage—they are the very best at what they do, measured by customer satisfaction and loyalty. Differentiated modules command high prices, high margins, and demonstrate excellent customer metrics. When the enterprise cannot deliver absolute advantage through internal specialization, it partners with external best-in-class providers via the low-cost partnering pathways of the global connectivity platform.

Responsiveness is achieved by listening to the customer's evolving and changing needs through social business software and business analytics, and quickly designing and implementing solutions to these evolving needs, so as to preserve differentiation and maintain loyalty. This responsiveness can be made rapid and objective via direct software connections to the customer. Mobile computing devices help ensure that the responsiveness is to universal rather than selective signals.

Efficiency is achieved by lowering costs across all business transactions and processes. The global connectivity platform provides a commodity low-cost platform, with no need to invest in customized IT, freeing up investment for differentiation. Social business software increases the efficiency of innovation by involving the customer in the process. Partnering with external best-in-class providers ensures that companies shed all but the most differentiated, highest margin value creation capabilities, and focus on maximizing their contribution.

Enterprise Level Social Business

The globally integrated enterprise is the future business model. IBM, for example, is committed to becoming a social business. IBM Connections is the social business software platform enabling many of its initiatives in this direction, and the platform is also available to IBM's customers. The software includes many of the elements you'd expect when you hear the term "social software": homepage, communities, blogging, crowdsourcing for ideation, bookmarks, activities, wikis, files, forums, and search. The software is componentized according to the service-oriented architecture concept, enabling customized assembly and very large-scale deployments.

IBM Developer Works is a professional networking site and technical resource center for software developers, running on the IBM Connections platform. It brings together hundreds of thousands of engineers and developers, and helps them develop and master relevant skills, collaborate with other engineers to solve problems, and to leverage the latest advances in open standards.

Entrepreneur Level Social Businesses

There are many ways that start-ups can access Glo-Mo-So and scale. To illustrate, we profile two very different regional small to medium enterprises in different fields that both serve children. Each has used many of the Service Thinking principles (although they may not have identified them as Service Thinking) to create new business models and have succeeded.

The iPhone and Android platforms have proliferated mobile access. But it may not be obvious what a dramatic difference the availability of these platforms can mean to something as important as healthcare and chronic disease management.

AsthmaMD has utilized Glo-Mo-So to transform disease management.

Asthma sufferers are a growing market: 18.9 million in the United States with 7.1 children among them. (file://localhost/(http/::www. cdc.gov:nchs:fastats:asthma.htm). Each year 1.2 million people in the United States visit hospital outpatient care departments with asthma as the primary diagnosis.[7]

Many chronic sufferers have a low compliance rate (inconsistently taking prescribed medication) and a poor understanding of their symptoms (leading to serious complications and trouble when symptoms get out of control). Proper monitoring and action, before an instance of the condition becomes critical, can enable the patient to avoid emergency hospitalization. Conventional doctor visits and medical procedures are inadequate to address these issues in an affordable, scalable way.

Dr. Sam Pejham, Pediatrician and Faculty in UCSF School of Medicine, has a special interest in asthma. While he might not consider himself a cutting edge entrepreneur in Service Thinking, his approach, analysis, and implementation empowered him and his team to be just that. They created the AsthmaMD App that now has 75,000 active users and is the largest mobile app for chronic disease management in the world, based on active users (not just downloads). Their goal is to be the #1 source for asthma for everything needed for patients, researchers, pharmaceutical companies, and caretakers.

Dr. Pejham recognized that increased mobile phone access has created a ubiquitous platform for timely medical information sharing with patients and data aggregation for researchers. Using mobile devices would make his service very scalable to any number of patients (no space constraints as in hospitals); it could be global to reach anyone, anywhere, anytime, and be automated so the professional interaction per use was not necessary.

The developers had no need of huge venture funding since mobile apps are not capital intensive. They assembled the right team: researchers, physicians, technologists, business people for funding, and patients.

They were not the first to apply a mobile app for asthma disease management, but they recognized what was missing. Their priority was not quick financial return on investment. The core value web was the patient–physician–researcher connection, sharing data, analytics, and activities between three communities that, heretofore, were not well integrated.

Patients can self-input and then share their information (they can opt out if they want to). There are five fields they can input—the more they put in, the greater the value to themselves, and the other stakeholders:

1. How they are feeling
2. Peak flow measurement
3. What medication they use (or plan to use)
4. Known asthma triggers
5. Notes they may enter

The mobile platform also provides immediacy of data gathering—at the point of suffering. A patient is unlikely to record symptoms, when they occur, with pen and paper, and they are unlikely to be sitting next to a computer. But many patients have a smartphone and can record an event immediately.

Physicians want to access and analyze this data to control asthma among their own patients; it helps their patients to understand their disease better, so they get better results from treatment. Active users have 10% improvement in pulmonary function results—as much as with inhaled cortico-steroids. In this sense, patient self-knowledge can be as good as medication—knowledge and understanding increases the opportunity to act before a critical situation occurs.

Researchers can aggregate data in new ways for new analytic insights. For example, they can compare asthma patients' daily inputs with known pollution data in different geographies, confirming, for example, the correlation of the levels of known pollutants like ozone with the level and characteristics of asthma symptoms. The integrity of the data sets and analytics has proven to be as good as controlled (and very expensive) National Institute of Health studies. A typical university study might be 30–50 people; AsthmaMD has 75,000 active users and can easily get data from 5 to 10,000 people.

The Business Model

In the case of AsthmaMD, the entrepreneurial team built a low-cost app, made it the best it can be, shared it freely with patients, and then recorded the data to demonstrate the improvement benefit. Once data was accumulated on tens of thousands of users, the entrepreneurs can shift gears into a monetization phase, with no loss of integrity (and, arguably, a gain):

- First, they were able to secure grants from organizations such as NIH, to further refine the platform and the research.
- Second, the scaled data sets and patient engagement attracted private enterprise such as health insurance companies wanting to advertise within the service, pharmaceutical companies seeking data, and medical device makers seeking association and endorsement.
- Third, the university medical school wants to support this kind of activity from its faculty.

Physicians are now "prescribing" AsthmaMD as a health solution for patients. New acquisitions are achieved through word of mouth from users and recommendations by professionals. AsthmaMD is now entering its exponential growth phase.

Steve & Kate's Camp has Utilized Glo-Mo-So to Scale Day Camp

While AsthmaMD is a social business built upon a technology platform, Steve & Kate's Camp illustrates how a small one-location business can scale to multiple locations (bricks and mortar in the form of rented schools for sites) through smarter use of technology applications with a great business model for co-creation of value. If you remember day camp as regimented, rigid time frames for limited scheduled activities (e.g., kickball, plastic lanyards, and popsicle stick and glue arts and crafts), then you are not hip to 21st century day camp.

Steve & Kate's Camp was started in 1980 by Steve and Kate Susskind, who had a simple idea as stated on their website, steveandkatescamp.com:

> *Instead of a rigid structure, we give our campers choice. Instead of teaching kids the typical way, we give them tools and gentle guidance to help them become autodidacts. The difference is subtle—and it's profound.*
>
> *At Steve & Kate's, campers step into a world packed with possibilities: for experiencing new sensations, for expressing themselves, for exploring their passions and potential. The results are unexpected and they're unexpectedly rich. One camper dives deep into stop-motion animation. Another discovers a passion for dance. Or chess. A camper becomes engrossed in making the ultimate spaghetti sauce. Or developing Leo Messi-like touch on the soccer pitch. These discoveries are all the more exhilarating because campers make them for themselves. This is a world liberated from adult judgments and expectations, and campers flourish in it.*
>
> *After 33 years, we're still 100 percent obsessed with making each edition of Steve & Kate's freer, fresher and more effective at inspiring campers to zero in on what makes them truly happy.*[8]

From 1980 until 2005, Steve & Kate's operated out of one location in Mill Valley, California. Since then they have adopted a systems approach that has enabled them to grow to eight sites in 2010, 18 sites in 2011, 26 sites in 2012, and 34 sites in 2013. They now serve tens of thousands of children each summer.

Ben Chun, the director of program design and research, has leveraged the Service Thinking concepts of co-development and co-elevation for Steve & Kate's.

1. The evolution of the platform itself: as the platform grows and transforms, new capabilities are added to support new types of services.
2. The innovation of services: by identifying, composing, and developing new services, emerging customer needs are met with existing platform capabilities.

When a camper arrives to the campsite, Steve & Kate's use a system to keep track of kids and who is authorized to pick them up; the registration is virtual at all locations and parents can choose which days to send their kids to camp. The company uses a Cloud-based system called Heroku, a service on top of Amazon. Virtualized, it can turn up and down the capacity, so it will adapt to any level of future geographic expansions.

Every parent has had the experience of asking a kid what he or she did at camping and hearing, "Nothing." So the company has innovated a solution. They have printed out wrist bands with QR codes (two-dimensional bar code). This allows anyone at camp to scan a camper's wristband and upload video/photos of what they are doing and attach a file to the child's individual account; end of day, parents can see the videos and photos in one e-mail sent to any device.

This provides a window into the world of what kids are doing when apart from their parents. It provides a great customer experience that is co-created by the provider (camp staff), the child who does the activities, and the parent who views them and can then send on to adoring grandparents and other family members anywhere.

Specialization and Integration Enables Scalable Growth

In addition to the technology that enables their systems to grow with no constraints, the company has solved the transport of all the rides, equipment, and supplies to each location through specialization and integration.

They use Pods storage containers, which is on demand storage. A Pod Company transports equipment to a warehouse for mini-storage (the camp sites are located in many different communities). To get everything needed on time to each location, they have the Pods storage logistics pros, who will schedule the drivers to drop and pick up at the right location with the right merchandise.

So Steve & Kate's management does not deal with trucking, storage, and warehousing logistics; they can ship larger orders (they may buy play structures from a central manufacturer) and will have staff at the Pod facility to direct where each container will go to each location, but never have to touch or transport the equipment.

These examples of regional small to medium sized businesses show that new business models, based on values-based companies that have strong customer co-development and co-elevation, can successfully scale—virtually as AsthmaMD or in bricks and mortar businesses as Steve & Kate's Summer Day Camps.

Glo-Mo-So will be one of the great equalizers to enable small businesses everywhere to exponentially scale without requisite large capital investments.

CHAPTER 6

Continuous Improvement Through Learning: Run-Transform-Innovate

Anyone who has never made a mistake has never tried anything new.
—Albert Einstein

Service Thinking embraces continuous improvement in service quality and service productivity. Customers are continuously searching for the best providers of top quality service experiences, and linking and delinking providers in their service system, aiming to better meet their goals or to do so with greater efficiency. Providers are continuously refining and elevating their value propositions in order to establish or maintain absolute advantage relative to competitors. They do so either via internal specialization, always adding to their specialized knowledge, or via external specialization, identifying specialists who can provide services more effectively or efficiently (perhaps innovative new start-ups), freeing up internal resources to further improve the value propositions that the producer's modularized business components are best at.

This continuous dynamic swirl of improvement can be a challenge to manage. It requires a culture that embraces the demands of continuous improvement stimulated by externalities—the preferences of the customer and the dynamic changes of the category and the market. And it requires a governance model that can allocate resources appropriately for an environment of continuous, dynamic, and occasionally disruptive change.

The New Governance Model

Such a governance model is rare in business. In fact, the norm is the opposite—favoring asset allocation and investments in maintaining the status quo. Geoffrey Moore eloquently and accurately identified the problem as "escaping the pull of the past."[1] The overwhelming tendency is for companies to focus their investment, effort, and people on maintaining the businesses that can reliably and predictably deliver quarterly revenues, margins, and earnings. Salespeople, marketers, operations, IT, finance, and all the major enterprise engines are dedicated to making those numbers with proven businesses, products, and services. Innovation tends to be underfunded and quickly abandoned if it does not deliver current period revenue and profit increments.

The result can often be stagnation (stuck in the same place in low growth markets) or even corporate failure—the enterprise is disrupted, surpassed, and replaced by an innovative solution from an unexpected source. Kodak is a prime example—a former industry leader that did not anticipate the full impact of the digital photography revolution and could not escape the pull of its historical highly profitable business model.

Service Thinking, properly applied, enables enterprises to escape the pull of the past. There are three reasons why:

1. Service systems have an inherent natural energy of continuous improvement. The service customer is continually asking, "How can I make my service experience better?" The customer evaluates all the service components in the service system in this light. If there is a constraint to greater productivity or service quality in the service system, the customer seeks to solve for that constraint, and works with the incumbent partner to co-create a resolution, or finds a replacement partner to co-create a new solution.[2] This energy is constantly flowing through service systems. Current providers and new aspiring providers are highly incented to improve.

2. Service Thinking uses analytical approaches to assess the opportunities for improvement in the service system, giving the service provider a tool to assess the current value proposition and identify the opportunities for new value co-creation. We'll visit these tools

in more detail in Chapter 8. The continuous improvement energy in the service system can be measured with the right analytics. The essence of the approach is continuous learning: running frequent experiments to learn how customers respond to new or enhanced value propositions, and rapidly transitioning to expanding the propositions that meet with the customer approval.

3. Because co-creation of value is the operative norm in service system productivity, the service provider and service customer are equally and effectively bound together in both the identification of service improvement opportunities and the innovation path to realizing the improvement. Both must analyze their constraints, both must make changes to achieve the improvement goals, and together they must collaborate; otherwise, new value will not be co-created. This symbiosis of service productivity is the reason why service science promises to achieve a new level of global productivity and value creation growth.

The enabling framework is in place but, as Geoffrey Moore would say, that in itself does not result in an escape from the pull of the past. Service systems require a governance model to guide investments to support the enabling framework; the model is Run-Transform-Innovate.

Run: Do More with Less

The first principle is to continuously free up investment from the task of maintaining and sustaining current operations and businesses. Efficiency in delivering proven value is the goal. This is not where new value is created, but the current value can be delivered at lower cost, with fewer people and fewer assets. The most ruthlessly competitive firms are continuously squeezing costs out of "Run" to transfer capital to "transform/innovate."

Transform: Enhance with Elevated Value Co-Creation

While the value co-creation level delivered via current operations and businesses can be maintained at high efficiency by doing more with less, improvement in quality and effectiveness is required to stay competitive. The continuous improvement energy of the service system means that businesses that are merely efficient will fall behind the ever-evolving standards of the service system. The Transform function is one of best practice adoption, constantly scanning the service system for emerging service improvements and adopting them quickly and applying them at Glo-Mo-So scale. In this mode, the enterprise is implementing the innovation of others for the good of the service system as a whole.

Innovate: Disrupt and Replace via New Value Co-Creation

Innovation is the creation of new value through new-to-the-world best practices and new-to-the-world solutions. It is high risk, and successes may be rare. However, the rewards in revenue and profit growth are substantial. Based on a study by Robert Litan, Vice President of Research and Policy at entrepreneurship-focused Kauffman Foundation, if 30–60 innovative, high-growth firms were launched every year in the United States of America, there would be a one percentage point increase in economy-wide GDP.[3]

The R-T-I Ratio

Leading practitioners of the Run-Transform-Innovate (RTI) governance model pay close attention to the ratio of the three components. Early in the decade of the 2000's, IBM's IT organization significantly shifted the percentage of its budget allocations; they reduced the allocation to "Run" by 10%, and shifted the freed-up resources toward "Transform and Innovate." The baseline was an analysis that the company was spending 73% of its IT budget on keeping systems and services running, and 27% on transformation/innovation. In 2009, the ratio was 63% allocated to "Run" and 37% to "Transform/Innovate." The goal is now to shift a further 2% from "Run" every year.

Some basic principles were applied to the job of run efficiency. One was simplification—for example, an organizational shift from 128 business CIOs to 1 enterprise CIO, and a reduction in applications from 15,000 apps to 4,500. Another was centralization—for example, consolidating 155 data centers into 5. Additional areas of cost reduction range from energy savings to business process simplification. The capability to massively reduce "Run" costs enables the shift of investment to "Transform/Innovate." IBM business managers have become highly skilled at operating on a 5% reduced budget compared to year ago—a massive contribution to the innovation success of the company. Reduced operating budgets and "Run" efficiencies become the norm and are embedded in the culture.

This also creates the opportunity for organizational innovation to play a bigger role. In addition to the "Run" organization that's responsible for keeping systems running smoothly at lower cost, IBM's IT department includes a "Transform" team focused on business process simplification and business transformation through the adoption of new best practices, and an "Innovate" unit that pursues new value-creating technology initiatives. The Transform and Innovate teams are empowered by the efficiency advances of the Run team and the R-T-I ratios can be shifted by a collaborative effort between the three teams.[4]

Geoffrey Moore cites the example of Akamai to illustrate the power of applying the R-T-I model. Akamai runs a network on top of the Internet to dynamically route and reroute traffic in order to minimize A-to-B point delays. In 2006, the company had an established core offering in the form of its content delivery network and an emerging technology platform called EdgeSuite used to accelerate interactive applications such as e-commerce. It was hard for the new technology to escape the investment pull of the dominant content delivery business.

To create the environment for change, Akamai reorganized from business units based on technologies to market-facing units built to serve vertical categories such as media and entertainment, and retail commerce. Then it regrouped its initiatives to align with the vertical categories, in a way that enabled the EdgeSuite technology to flourish. Content delivery was the core business (equivalent to "Run") and was particularly appropriate for the media and entertainment vertical. Two new businesses represented the "Transform" initiatives, based on the EdgeSuite technology: Dynamic Site Acceleration focused on serving retail commerce customers, and Web Application Acceleration focused on serving enterprise CIO's supporting remote mobile applications running over the public Internet. A third new business based on a novel technology ("Innovate") focused on serving advertisers seeking better yields from web-based campaigns.

With these new initiatives appropriately organized into R-T-I groupings and aligned with target verticals, Akamai was able to direct investment to shift the R-T-I ratio. The result was growth in the new businesses which, combined, eventually surpassed the total revenues in the core content delivery business.

Similarly, IKEA's supply chain management boasts a number of operational (i.e., "Run") efficiencies. For example, the company reduced transportation costs and enhanced transportation capacity by implementing best practices like flat-packed products. Flat-packed benefits included not only increased storage capacity in warehouses, but also reduced construction costs and reduced inventory losses through damage, as per a business essay on UKEssays.com.[5] Operational efficiencies were also introduced through the implementation of a "Demand Planning" and "Replenishment Planning" platform ("Transform"). The implementation helped IKEA in quicker and more accurate decision making and forecasting, besides a significant reduction in inventory carrying costs.

Burberry Group PLC is another good example of the breakthrough growth opportunities that become available when cost-reduction from operational efficiencies ("Run") are invested in transformative innovation. It is among the most efficient in its industry at managing inventories, with only 183.23 days of cost of goods sold tied up in inventory, compared to an industry benchmark. The retailer invested 60% of its annual marketing budget in becoming a digital brand, connected with its consumers across all devices ("Innovate"). In 2012, for the second consecutive year, the brand earned the No. 1 spot in L2 Digital IQ Index®: Fashion. One of its innovative strategies includes offering digital product customization for its customers via its microsite "Burberry Bespoke," shareable across social media channels like Facebook and Twitter. Multichannel strategy is emphasized via digital in-store integration. Some Burberry merchandise now carries RFID chips for customers interested in more information and full-length screens at its Regent Street store in London stream visual content while doubling up as mirrors.[6]

Commenting on Home Depot's acquisition of Black Locus, a start-up that develops pricing and other algorithms to help retailers optimize their web sales, Hal Lawton, SVP at Home Depot, made a clear statement of the R-T-I principle. "Gone are the days where we're building 50–200 stores a year," he said. "We're shifting that capital to technology that can help us advance our business at a much faster pace.[7]"

Mayo Clinic is another good example of R-T-I. Mayo initiated learning about the transition to a paperless system by implementing a hospital management software from an obscure vendor, Cerner. By 1998 the clinic had entirely eliminated paper from its out-patient department. Mayo spent $16 million on medical practice automation over the first 5 years of operation and has realized savings of $3 million to $7 million annually thereafter.[8]

Transforming Government with R-T-I

Federal, state, and local governments are realizing that they have the same opportunity to run more with less.

Craig Newmark, founder of Craig's list, is a keen champion of e-government and e-citizenship. He has noted some of the changes in government operations that incorporate many of the Cloud-based best practices, including specialization and integration, we have been advocating for enterprises. Here is what he has to say about VistA:

> VistA is the Department of Veterans Affairs health record system, and it's been a huge success. VA has open sourced it, which is a remarkable achievement for Washington, a really big deal. It means that anyone can improve it or interface with it. Check out the Challenge.gov VA Medical Appointment Scheduling Contest.
>
> What they're now saying is that the Department of Defense is considering a health records system, and that VistA should be considered for that.
>
> That sounds right to me, it gets the job done, has been working well for years, and is already available publicly to better help veterans. That means people can find ways to add function to better help active service troops.[9]

The expanding adoption of R-T-I may be the opening market opportunity for many entrepreneurs and specialists, who might think that large multinational corporations and governments are too rigid and cumbersome to be open to innovation, to apply for contracts to serve the larger customer base these entities can offer.

CHAPTER 7

Multisided Metrics

You can tell what is important in an organization by what they measure.

—Mohamed Yunus

Metrics are developed from the objectives and goals statements in the enterprise strategy model. They measure the success of the enterprise in achieving its goals. Traditionally, metrics have focused on outputs such as revenue and profit growth, number of customers served, productivity per employee, and so forth.

While the Service Thinking enterprise seeks to make revenue and profit goals just like a traditional enterprise, it embraces qualitative objectives and goals as well. The output of a service is an experience and is perceived subjectively by the customer. The Service Thinking enterprise must address the challenge of measurement in the era of subjectivity. The degree of the customer's engagement in co-creation is a determinant of the provider's success. The Service Thinking enterprise must tackle the concept of shared responsibility for value production. These new characteristics of the Service Thinking enterprise demand a new approach to measuring business success.

Service Metrics for Engagement and Duration

In co-creation of value, customers contribute and participate by injecting their resources, applying their competencies, and communicating their preferences and needs, so the producer may respond. There must be active engagement.

Consider the digital app Fitbit in the personal health field that tracks a customer's performance in calories consumed, miles run, or paces walked. If the customer does not engage in the "digital work" of consistently collecting and reporting the data, the provider cannot deliver on the value proposition of tracking, projecting, benchmarking, encouraging, and rewarding.

The customer engagement extends over time; it is not a single transaction. Rather, it is an evolving and maturing relationship. Snapshot-in-time metrics are unable to capture such a relationship. If a Fitbit customer signs up, logs in, and reports on calories consumed for one day, a snapshot report would indicate a customer acquisition and transaction; however, no real value is created if the customer does not continue to provide information over an extended period of time.

Multisided Metrics Replace One-Sided Metrics

Traditional revenue, profit, share, and transaction volume metrics are "Pulse" measures—they measure the pulse of the business. As such they are useful in tracking mechanical and financial performance, but they cannot capture the value co-creation dynamics of service. How effective is the enterprise in inducing customers to apply their resources, competencies, and efforts to co-creating with the producer? How effective is the enterprise in maintaining this relationship? How does the customer perceive the experience of co-creation and how does that perception advance or decline over time? Service Thinking organizations must search for the right metrics to answer these questions.

Longer Term Rather Than Shorter Term

American business has often been criticized for a focus on short-term measures such as quarterly and annual revenues and earnings. Short-term metrics sometimes undermine long-term focus. Service Thinking has an emphatic bias toward the longer term. Addressing the issue of short-term versus long-term priorities is one of the key purposes of the Run-Transform-Innovate model for input allocation. Similarly, business outcome metrics should reinforce the long-term bias. Service experiences are often developed over time. Desirable service results such as reliability, consistency, and meeting customer expectations cannot be judged on a one-time transaction; rather they require an extended period (perhaps multiple years) before they mature.

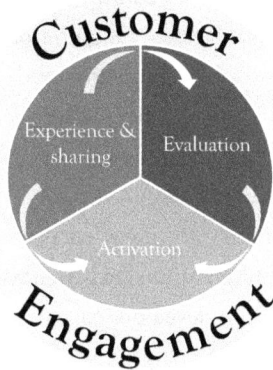

Figure 7.1. Customer engagement pathway.

We expect that businesses will continue to report short-term financial and trading results to investors and stock analysts (although the first signs of resistance to this pressure are beginning to show at companies like Google and Amazon). We will focus here on the metrics with the most promise for long-term service productivity improvement.

The Path to Service Success

Customer engagement is best viewed as a pathway: dynamic, iterative, and evolving in a longer term relationship. There are three main stages along the path:

- Evaluation—the customer experiences a need, perhaps unmet or poorly met in his or her current service system, and is evaluating the value proposition of a new or replacement service. The customer may also be in an unsatisfactory provider relationship and is considering changes or switching.
- Activation—this could be trial, re-trial, or ongoing loyal purchase and represents the commitment of the customer to actively engage with the offering; in some business models, there is no purchase of the service itself (such as using Google's free search engine service) but the customer does commit to exposure to advertising and other monetization techniques.

- Experience and sharing—the output of a service is an experience, which is multifaceted, ranging from the functional experience ("it works," "it meets my need," or "it doesn't work for me") to the emotional experience ("I feel good about this service," "I love it!" or "I am disappointed," "I hate it!"). Perhaps the greatest new change in the science of service metrics is the impact of sharing the experience; customers share both their functional and emotional experiences with others in all kinds of forums, from developer communities commenting on software bugs, and share groups comparing their experiences with a common supplier, to ratings on Amazon and commentary on Facebook or Yelp! This high-impact variable demands measurement and tracking.

The Gateway to the Path: Insights

In Human Action, Ludwig von Mises ascribes all economic advancement to the "purposive human"—people "aiming at certain ends and motivated by the urge to improve their state of satisfaction"[1] This is a good place for Service Thinking to start. We need first to understand the motivation of customers: what are they aiming for and which elements of their state of satisfaction do they desire to improve.

Von Mises believed that all human action is individual action. He therefore anticipated the economics of individualization—an inherent implication of Service Thinking, since customization, co-creation, and co-elevation drive inexorably toward better individualization of the service experience.

Motivation is difficult to measure, since it is both qualitative and subjective. If we ask a customer to identify his or her motivation, it is unlikely we will get an accurate answer. What we can do is generate an insight, which is the provider's understanding of the customer's motivation. Insights can be derived from research data, and the most valuable route is to observe and measure *behavior* and, from that, derive motivation. The promise of "Big Data" is that analytical tools can be applied to high volume, high velocity, and high variability data sets: clickstreams, shopping cart and checkout data, repeat purchases, club membership, participation in ratings and rankings, online community participation, blogging, and commenting. Armed with this information, the astute provider can then hypothesize and calibrate the motivations that drive the behavior:

> *The first multisided metric we recommend for the service-centric enterprise is: Are we generating insights? Do we have a competency in collecting behavioral data and analyzing it for sentiment (i.e., the emotional driver behind the action), and identifying the motivation of the customer that the sentiment reveals?*

A necessary corollary of the capability to generate insights is the ability to identify customer segments. A value proposition can never be relevant to 100% of the market, since different customers will have different motivations. In the smartphone market, some customers will be motivated by their drive for maximum achievement to acquire and use a full-featured iPhone, and some others might be driven by their desire to be smart shoppers by carefully identifying only the features that they need and selecting a limited set of features for a lower price. These emotions (need for achievement, need for feeling smart) are the variables in a segmentation schema of the target customers in the smartphone market. In generating insights, the enterprise should focus on insights into its own target customers and their motivations. The enterprise with deeper insights, and deeper understanding of the target customer, will be the more successful in developing a winning value proposition and establishing relationship loyalty:

> *The second metric we recommend is a measure of the value of the insights. A value is a function of the number of customers covered by the insight, the likelihood of action to convert them to a desired behavior, and the value to the enterprise of that behavior.*

Let's say that we offer a service that enables customers to track their dietary actions and the calories and nutrients that they intake, along with their caloric expenditure in exercise activities. It is extremely likely that we could identify the motivations of potential customers from big data sets (content to which they subscribe or which they read, apps they use, and activities they pursue). We should also be able to accurately estimate how many individuals share this motivation, and what proportion of them might subscribe to our new service that improves their ability to achieve their motivational goal. If we add an estimate of the economics of subscription (either in service subscription fees, advertising to subscribers, or sales of associated products to subscribers), then we can place a value on our insight. As a result, we can prioritize across multiple insights and focus our R-T-I investments on those with the highest potential.

The enterprise should have a portfolio of high value insights and an R-T-I strategy to invest in them in order to monetize them in the marketplace.

Business Architecture for Insights

There is clearly interplay between quantitative methods (data collection, data processing, analytics, and modeling) and qualitative understanding (customer perceptions, motivations, and experiences) in the generation of insights. Businesses are linking the IT management of data collection, storage, and analytics with human-centric Service Thinking.[2] The CIO of Procter & Gamble renamed IT "Information and Decision Solutions" for precisely that reason—to shift the focus of IT to facilitating better evidence-based decisions.[3]

But even the best-implemented IT system installations can prove to be opaque to thoughtful development of insights, because they can't cope with the kind of qualitative queries that often characterize Service Thinking, or they can't flex with changing customer segments or trends in sentiment.

In fact, a Componentized Business Architecture approach can be applied to generate architecture to ensure that the business value of information and insights is not lost in IT rigidities.[4]

Table 7.1 Illustrates a simplified description of the appropriate architecture. The key implication is that IT must be a service system for business components (in this example, the Customer strategy component) and must provide a measurable service output (results from activities that generate a growing insights portfolio value and actionable service innovation).

Now let's relate this to our three-stage Customer Engagement Pathway

Stage 1: Evaluation

Customers are conscious of the opportunity to improve their service experience and are seeking information on their choices. They have a

Table 7.1. Gateway Metrics and Business Architecture

Gateway Metrics	
Artifact	Insights
Metric	Size and growth of insights portfolio; value of insights portfolio
Information entity	Customer segment
Architecture	
Business component	Customer strategy
Process	Insights generation
Quality required	Results in actionable service innovation
Activities	Data collection, analytics, and modeling
Instrumentation	Analytical and modeling software
Infrastructure	Data storage and processing; analytical interface

lot of resources including reviews and ratings of both B2C and B2B services, professional and amateur commentary, analyses of features and attributes, web sites, Facebook pages, Twitter tracks, special interest communities, social sharing sites such as Pinterest, and countless digital records.

The multisided metrics an enterprise pursues in this stage must focus on consonance: are we demonstrating potential to fit into the customer's service system in order to be considered. In a service system, consonance is the quality of an entity's value proposition that enables the opportunity to co-create value with others. A good way to think of consonance is captured in the idea of "fitting in." The entity seeking to participate in the service system must understand the needs of the customer who has assembled the service system with a view to achieving specific end benefits and must demonstrate attributes and offerings consistent with the customer, the benefits sought and the system that has already been assembled.

The quest to establish consonance is itself a source of innovation. For example, in marketing and brand building the historical norm has been the assertive claim of the brand to iconic or superior status. Consonant brands are much more humble, seeking first to understand and to establish the potential for value by fitting in rather than by making assertive claims. It is the search for consonance that has elevated areas of the service offering such as environmental sensitivity and social responsibility. *To fit into the customer's service system, it is necessary to share and support the customer's values.*

Once the prospective service provider has demonstrated sufficient alignment with customer values and understanding of customer context, the opportunity is open to demonstrate resonance, that is, the co-creation of superior value. This requires a new, different, or better value proposition than currently exists in the service system, motivating customers to commit their own resources to the co-creation opportunity, and welcoming the new provider or new offering into the service system.

The metrics of consonance can be derived from the same sources as we have already identified: customer sentiment and customer behavior.

Service Equity

Brand equity is a term used in marketing to signify a bundle of perceptions held by both brand users and non-users that constitute the "image" of the brand, especially relative to other brands in the category, in the mind of category customers. While the metric is qualitative, subjective, and emotional, it can nevertheless be measured on a scale (e.g., a score on a 10-point scale given by the customer to indicate their perception of the fit between a desired attribute and the brand's delivery of that attribute) and mapped on a perceptual grid compared to other brands in the category. It can also be tracked over time to ascertain whether perceptions are strengthening or weakening relative to other brands. In B2B, the idea of brand equity is often subsumed in the definition of the value proposition. It is equally important to apply metrics to value propositions—for example Sonoco, in the early 2000's was able to link the metrics of DVPs (Distinctive Value Propositions) directly to growth in top-line revenues and EBIT.[5]

In Service Thinking, we utilize service equity as a measure of consonance. The metric is developed via survey and/or via sentiment analysis, based on the answer to customized questions such as:

- Do you consider this service offering from this provider as a qualified offering in your consideration set?

- Do you believe this service offering meets your needs?
- I respect this service provider (Yes/No or scale response).
- This provider's values are consistent with those of my company (Yes/No or scale response).

The status of service equity should be gathered with regular data collections and reports and tracked on a longitudinal basis. Service equity tracking data can be correlated with business metrics such as revenue growth, customer acquisitions and defections, and market share, but the relationship is not directly causal.

Stage 2: Activation

Acquisition and Retention

With evaluation completed to a stage sufficient to support a decision, the customer moves to the activation stage: sampling, trying, joining, or subscribing to the service. The metrics of activation are straightforward. The goal is to measure the stream of activation and its quality. Activation quality can comprise:

- Level: do new acquisitions enter at the minimum level of commitment (e.g., using the minimum number of features or accepting the lowest subscription level) or do significant proportions enter at a premium level. Do they commit for a minimum period of time or longer?
- Depth: do new acquisitions immediately or very quickly become engaged with multiple levels of the offering and use multiple features? Do they engage in co-creation? Do a large number of members of their organization quickly adopt the new service? Do they use social features and quickly make connections to other users?
- Loyalty dynamics: do acquisitions translate into long-term loyal customers? Does the level of usage escalate? What are attrition rates, and are they stable or improving or worsening? Do loyal users bring in new users?

At this stage on the path, we are focused on behavioral metrics—what customers do? When we are certain that we have a strong grasp of behavior, we can transition to metrics of understanding.

Stage 3: Experience and Sharing

Value Creation Experience: Resonance

Experience metrics are measures of innovation and superior delivery—we use the term *resonance* to indicate that the customer experienced the value they anticipated at Stage 2. In assembling their service system to achieve their ends, customers were seeking both functional and emotional benefits. Functionally, they were looking for services that deliver desired benefits in a superior way—lower cost, faster, more reliable, more accurate, easier to use and access, even, perhaps, more elegantly. Emotionally, they were seeking to achieve a desired feeling. For a CIO purchasing technical services, that feeling could be one of confidence, or it could be one of competence, or it could be one of competitive superiority. For a father purchasing ballet lessons for his daughter, the feeling could be one of family togetherness or feeling like a great dad. It is critical to understand the emotional benefits of service in the metrics of resonance.

In survey data or sentiment tracking for customer experience, the measurement lies in customer ratings or rankings for "best," "most innovative," "most efficient," or "competitively superior." In quantifying resonance on a scale, it is possible to compute both an absolute score (e.g., 90 on a 100-point scale for "efficient") and distance versus competitors (e.g., 30 points higher on the same scale for the same benefit). To maintain its value creation status, a company may set resonance benchmarks for its service offerings, for example, MUST score at least 85 on a 100-point scale for a selected benefit, and MUST show at least 20-point superiority on that scale versus the nearest competitor. With this combination of high absolute score and clear distance versus competition, the resonant value creation status is confirmed.

If customer experience metrics indicate below-target performance, there may be a "customer gap"[6]—a difference between customer expectations and customer experience. It can be a design gap—the service is not adequately designed to meet the customer's expectations—or a delivery gap—the service is designed adequately but not implemented to the level of the design.

A high satisfaction score on a survey can be taken as a declaration that the service met customer expectations. The score should be trended over time and compared to some known benchmark of excellence. For example, a provider may set 80% satisfaction (at least 8.0 on a 10-point scale) as a minimum threshold. This satisfaction level should be correlated with a behavioral loyalty measurement to ensure that it is consistent with a high level of repeat usage and a low level of defection. Satisfaction is sentiment, loyalty is behavior. Providers must continually monitor the link between the two to make sure it is robust.

Second-level diagnostics can identify the source of the gaps, such as a poor service development process for a design gap, or an inadequate service personnel training for a delivery gap.

The path becomes a closed loop when customers share their sentiments about their service experience in the many formats and forums available for them to do so, on the Internet. Their experience sharing becomes the data that new evaluators use in Stage 1 of the path in their evaluations. Monitoring and, insofar as possible, managing the sharing of sentiment becomes a crucial activity for service providers.

Positive/Negative Sentiment Monitoring

Data analytics now make it possible to track customer sentiment regarding the service experience, and how that sentiment is being shared in digital forums. The analysis can take the form of a simple positive/negative tally. It can go deeper and draw insights about the drivers of these sentiments, and whether any negatives are a design gap or performance gap issue.

Customer Advocacy

One of the most productive acts of co-creation in the Glo-Mo-So environment is the advocacy of the service by one customer to another. As customers strive to maximize the value creation in their service system, expert opinion is less valuable than the actual experience of peers who have preceded them. When a customer recommends the provider of a service experience to another potential customer, this act leads to business growth and reinforced loyalty for the provider brand.

In B2C, first-time mothers are especially responsive to the recommendations of experienced mothers who have preceded them along the child-rearing path. When the experienced mother recommends a brand of diaper or a toy that encourages educational play patterns, the first-time mothers are highly likely to take the advice if they are connected to the advocate in a social community. Diaper brand, Huggies has used Facebook efficiently for this purpose. Its website www.huggies.com/mommyanswers caters to questions that to-be or new mothers tend to have. These questions can be posted on Huggies' Facebook wall too, for the community to answer. In fact, on approaching one million fans, the brand had also started a promotion, where for every piece of parenting advice shared by the community, a diaper would be donated to a baby in need.

In B2B, it is common practice in tech conventions for software providers to invite customer CEOs and CIOs to make presentations to the convention attendees to tell their customer satisfaction stories.

The value of customer advocacy lies behind the Net Promoter Score.[7] This is a metric based on the percentage of customers allocating a score of 9 or 10 on a 10-point scale in answer to the question "How likely are you to recommend this service to a friend?," minus the percentage who are detractors (allocating a score of less than 6). A positive score (more advocates than detractors) is associated with strong marketplace success.

To see how multisided metrics can be applied, we profile Bunchball, a service provider utilizing the combination of business analytics and gamification to measure and influence employee engagement and customer loyalty.

Bunchball, founded by Rajat Paharia, is a start-up that has grown to become a medium-sized enterprise. One of their products, an IBM Connections onboarding system called "Level Up," has scaled and enabled Bunchball to add quality content to a wide number of IBM partners. Bunchball defines Service Thinking principles as well as demonstrates the power of Glo/Mo/So with multisided metrics as its core business strategy. Bunchball is in the business of measuring and moving customer and employee engagement with the integration of big data and gamification. Its system can specialize and integrate into any industry and enterprise, so Bunchball can become a component in the business architecture.

(For more detail on Bunchball please check out this YouTube video http://www.youtube.com/watch?v=rro5G0yLyeE and Rajat Paharia's book: Loyalty 3.0: http://loyalty30.com

The Opportunity to Improve Employee Engagement and Customer Loyalty

Employee disengagement is a major problem in the workplace. According to Gallup surveys,[11] 70% of employed Americans are not engaged in their jobs.

Paharia suggests much of this dissatisfaction is due to a pervasive feeling (measured via sentiment analysis) that employees do not have autonomy and do not feel appreciated. Bunchball has developed methods to monitor and improve employee satisfaction through understanding employee motivation and then using gamification to motivate behavior change and create a more employee friendly work structure.

While gamification in business has become a hot trend, enterprises should be careful in how to integrate gamification into their business. Gartner predicts that, "by 2015, 40% of Global 1000 organizations will use gamification as the primary mechanism to transform business... by 2014, 80% of current gamified applications will fail to meet business objectives, primarily due to poor design.[12]"

Bunchball has an impressive track record in aligning business objectives for employee engagement and customer loyalty with their gamification and Big Data proprietary systems.

While employee satisfaction and engagement is important, every enterprise wants to increase the loyalty of its customer base. Bunchball uses metrics to help achieve this goal. Paharia calls this Loyalty 3.0: empower the business to motivate, to engage, and to create true loyalty by combining the latest research on human motivation, with generated big data by customers, partners, and employees as they interact with the provider.

One way to do this is to take the behaviors/attitudes of the best customers/employees and use the activity data to profile top users and then encourage those who are at lower levels to do the same activities. For example, if top employee performers are watching a lot of instructional videos that improve performance, then enterprise could gamify to encourage instructional video usage by others. Both USA Network and MTV modeled their top users and used that to figure out what behaviors they should try to motivate in their lower tiers of users.

Using multisided metrics can increase the perceived value of the enterprise. The SAP Community Network has developed a reputation system for the greater public good that helps the community and the individual in his/her career. Whomever has a higher reputation by points earned in the community bestows good reputation for career.

Gamification can also co-create value with customers. Kraft Canada http://firsttaste.kraftcanada.com/ rewards customers who cook and share recipes for all kinds of rewards, engaging the gamified community to get better insights with customers and valuable feedback.

Bunchball uses the peer-to-peer communications about the company and its products as a strategic competency; it has become even more important in some cases than the company's generated communications. Social media has changed the power dynamic. Recent Nielsen studies show that 92% of consumers trust a peer recommendation, compared to a 29%–47% trust rate for a company advertisement.[8]

At the core of Bunchball's business value proposition, Paharia's insight is understanding human motivation and then connecting big data and gamification to measure and change engagement based on those insights. He cites Forrester Research,[9] where they define engagement as having three parts:

- A deep emotional connection with the brand
- High levels of active participation
- A long-term relationship.

He states, "Note the point about active participation—engaged constituents don't just feel, they act. They participate, advocate, ideate, contribute, and generally engage in high level activity that makes your business better. What this definition makes clear is that the path to true loyalty is through engagement.[10]"

This level of employee and customer engagement is the goal of customer value co-creation. Bunchball has been able to "bottle it" and bring it to implementation.

Summary

In the Service Thinking approach to metrics, IT and customer facing functions collaborate to

- generate insights;
- support positive evaluations by customers;
- monitor and manage customer activations;
- monitor, manage, and maximize the customer experience;
- monitor and manage experience sharing.

CHAPTER 8

Applying Service Thinking for Innovation

If you do not change direction, you may end up where you are heading.

—Lao Tzu

The dynamic interactions of Service Thinking foundation concepts can lead to revolutionary industry and enterprise disruptions. We can map how such transformations might take place, all the while retaining the strategic humility to recognize that ultimate outcomes are emergent and not subject to prediction.

Can You Imagine the Unimaginable?

We can look backwards and see how value was co-created and co-evolved with social Internet technology to facilitate the emergence of user-generated communities such as Facebook. Can we imagine the future to envision what is not yet here, in a field in which the technology has arrived, but the processes of co-evolution and co-elevation are yet to be developed?

Let's look at 3D printing. According to Wikipedia, this recent technology facilitates the individual manufacture of three-dimensional solid objects from a digital model.[1] It makes hardware out of software; it renders the tangible from the intangible. 3D printing can produce jewelry and art, dental devices, automobile parts, tools, and many more items. People paid attention when the makers of the successful 2012 James Bond movie "Skyfall" hired a 3D printing supplier to make 3D replica 1965 Aston Martin DB5's, suitable for strafing with machine gun fire and blowing up without damaging the original.[2] The technology has proven functional.

How will 3D printing emerge from its current status as a specialist/hobbyist novelty to achieve the "third industrial revolution" that some are predicting for it? Let us trace the virtuous circle.

Value Co-Creation

One entry point for 3D printing is co-creation. Much of the early development and exploration has taken place within the free and open source software space. Because of this relatively open license environment, it has been easy for hobbyists to share designs and ideas, and it is easy for them to invent new variants of 3D printers. The hobbyist and early adopter community can collaboratively advance the technology and its applications. And significant progress has been made into value creation in business. For example, special parts can be designed and rapidly manufactured through 3D printing, such as hinges and other components for kitchen cupboards and fixtures, and custom shaped parts for the assembly of planes and cars. The designer supplies a digital specification for the part, and the 3D printing software translates this into machine instructions, and the new part is co-created. The evolutionary direction points to a future that is solidly in the center of significant value creation in the global economy.

Componentization

Another stage in service transformation will be the componentization of the architecture for the delivery and consumption of 3D printing service experiences.

How can we build substantial consonance and resonance? 3D printing would have to become as easy for customers as printing on paper. We can easily buy printers from HP, Kyocera, and others, either at retail stores or online. We can download printer drivers if we need to, and we can order ink supplies. It's easy to replace ink cartridges, and we are alerted when ink is low and seamlessly directed to online ordering, with next day delivery, if we require it. We can buy paper, in sizes that we know will fit industry-standard paper trays. Software that we run on our computers, laptops, smartphones, and tablets can all generate a print command in order to output a printed page. We can choose to buy branded ink cartridges or less expensive unbranded forms that fit into our printers in the same way as the proprietary versions (making the choice to forego the feelings of trust and confidence that come with the brand experience). We can have them delivered via standardized services from UPS or FedEx— just check the appropriate box and the details are all taken care of. If we don't want to print in our own offices, we can send the print instructions to FedEx Office or another external specialized printing capability.

These standardized interfaces and well-established protocols illustrate the componentization of the printing industry. There is a value web of component manufacturing resources to make parts for assembly into printers of varying capabilities, customizable from standard parts into a printing service that fits individual customer needs. There are standard formulas for ink and paper so that we can rely upon the performance of these components of the printing experience. Software interfaces are intuitive; when we pull down the "File" menu and choose "Print," we can be confident of the outcome (and we can easily change the settings if we choose to). Reliable componentized code has been developed for these functions, with the IP protected in such a way as to make usage widely available. Delivery components, courtesy of specialists such as UPS and FedEx, are integrated into the organization of the printing ecosystem.

This componentization of 3D printing has not yet evolved, but it is on its way. STL file formats are becoming a universal standard and can interface with CAD and modeling software. The colors and performance standards for the printing "inks" are evolving, so that output can be standardized and be capable of meeting expectations without excessive variability. There is not yet a Kyocera or an HP of 3D printers, but one will emerge when the industry size becomes big enough to attract these standardizing firms. There is no established destination on the web to go to in order to browse a list of available designs for printed components like hinges and brackets or plastic panels; perhaps amazon.com will provide this service, or maybe an industrial cataloguer like Grainger. The printers themselves have not yet evolved to the point where they become "plug and play" on any network, attachable to a standard MacBook or Dell laptop, and accessible from Lion OS or Windows 8, or via a downloadable app from the App Store.

Componentization will lower costs and increase the speed of adoption of the technology. It will enable big players like HP to decide whether or not to add the appropriate capabilities to enter the 3D printing industry, and to integrate with parts suppliers and channels of distribution.

Glo-Mo-So

3D printing will be plugged into an appropriate Glo-Mo-So platform. Ordering printers and parts, exchange of CAD designs and files, click-to-print on Macs, and Windows-based devices will all be seamlessly enabled. Diffusion will accelerate. Apps will be designed, written and offered to simplify access to and use of the 3D printing process. Printing hubs will probably emerge first (such as specially equipped FedEx Office locations or even more complex 3D printing specialist shops) but eventually, 3D printers will proliferate on the edges of private and public networks, just like paper printers.

Here is an example of how Glo-Mo-So and componentization have already inspired new businesses unimaginable before.

Makerbot Doll houses made through 3D printing from CAD produced design sets from Kacie Hulgren a theatre set designer: http://www.makerbot.com/blog/2012/04/23/mbtv-s02e08-scenic-design/

Service Systems

The 3D printing service system will take shape. Value-in-use has been established. However, value-in-experience is not yet substantially developed.

3D printing does not yet easily fit in to current service systems (i.e., has not established consonance) and has not yet demonstrated how it can be employed to co-create massive amounts of new value for a large number of people and entities (i.e., has not established resonance).

From the Makerbot Doll Houses using 3D printing illustrated above, let's consider a more traditional offering in the same toy industry, Thomas the Tank Engine, to illustrate how legacy brands could be transformed with Service Thinking using 3D printing and other adjacent possibilities.

Case Example: Thomas the Tank Engine Opportunity Using Service Thinking

Let us speculate, for example, that a toy company, observing the emergence of a componentized capability supported by Glo-Mo-So platform standards, and possibly collecting data about the gifting of 3D printers among early adopter communities, makes the decision to integrate 3D printing into the service system of "child's play." We could imagine, for example, that one of our childhood favorite toy characters, Thomas The Tank Engine, enters the world of 3D printing. It would be perfectly in character, since Thomas already embraces printed books, a TV show, CDs, apps, web content, games, clothing, and accessories, as well as toys ranging from individual engines to play sets for assembly.

What if the Thomas brand were to offer parents of young children who have already entered the Thomas franchise the opportunity to extend and deepen the Thomas experience by 3D printing new engines, new pieces of track, and new accessories like engine sheds and tunnels? Mattel (the owner of the Thomas brand) could market a piece of CAD software or an app to its current owners and community members, downloadable to a laptop computer or smartphone. The customer would pay for the app and, with a suitable standard interface for customizing and personalizing colors and characterization (via a list of choices within the software), 3D print the items in their own home, and plug the printed items into their existing play-sets. Perhaps a Mattel approved integrated partner would supply the "inks." If the customer did not already own a 3D printer, Mattel would refer them to another preferred partner in the ecosystem.

Now a service system has emerged on both the provider and customer sides of co-creation. The provider's system includes integrated specialists aligned around the provider goal of extending and strengthening the Thomas brand franchise and delivering an innovative customer brand experience, expanding a trust that has already been built. On the customer side of the service system, consonance results from the established propensity for the Thomas brand to extend into contemporary forms of experience. Resonance results from an integration of a totally new way of parents and children experiencing the pleasure of being a Thomas fan. The social sharing that takes place among children will rapidly validate the new function and expanded benefits of the brand. Parental connections will result in them sharing new adaptations and experiments with the Thomas 3D printing experience, and new bursts of co-creation and new forms of value-in-use will occur. Value-in-experience becomes established; in our example, the experience is an established one of the parent–child experience of play, a context with a valuable global marketplace.

Now, both the 3D printer companies (like HP in our hypothetical example) and the experience designers (like Mattel in our even more hypothetical example) can look to their R-T-I ratios and decide whether and how to allocate more resources to the transformation and innovation of the customer experience, in the context of the emerging demand for 3D printing experiences. Adding 3D printers to the HP offering and a 3D printing experience to the Thomas brand offering required an "I" form of resource allocation. Both companies will have found places in their portfolio of expenditures and activities to squeeze some resources out of "R" budgets in order to facilitate the new offerings and will be incented by the market to continue with the transformation.

They will be aided in making these resource allocation decisions by their analytics and KPIs. The multisided metrics for HP will measure the behaviors of customers in ordering new printers and "inks", and their usage levels—infrequent and occasional or regular and increasing. On the sentiment side, are they expressing satisfaction with the experience? Are they advocating to others? Is the blogosphere sentiment positive or negative? Are there reviews on Yelp? Has Amazon.com become a major online destination for the purchase of printers and accessories and materials?

How does the 3D printing category compare with the paper-printing category? Is Walmart in the service system yet?

For Mattel, there will be the metrics of unit sales, of course, but also whether or not this form of innovation reinforces the Thomas brand image. On the scale of "most loved by children," has this new feature moved the score upwards? Are children socially sharing the experience with peers, and are parents doing so with other parents? Are new co-created ideas being discussed in Thomas forums? Are the early signals that characterize the pathway to broad adoption found in the responses to the new Thomas offering?

This is all pure speculation. But our thought experiment has shown how Service Thinking can, conceivably, identify a robust pathway to a new and profitable field of value creation. In this case, once co-creation in an open source arena gains a foothold, the critical pivot point is whether the industry can componentize, both by establishing new standards and interfaces, and by integrating with componentization that has already taken place in areas like Asian component manufacturing networks and componentized coding of software. Soon afterwards, or perhaps contemporaneously, 3D printing scales and diffuses via a Glo-Mo-So platform, integrating software devices and networks that facilitate global adoption. Then, established service systems start to bring 3D printing into important everyday contexts (we used "Parent–Child Play" as an established experiential context in our hypothetical example). New experiences will also emerge with a new integrated service system—perhaps a new form of collectable art, or printable furniture or buildings. Finally, firms will look to re-balance their R-T-I (Run-Transform-Innovate) resource allocation ratios in order to achieve speed and critical mass in the new emerging service system and will develop the analytics, KPIs and models to shape and direct their investments and stay on the leading edge of a rapidly developing disruption.

We must emphasize nonlinearity. Service Thinking incorporates the capability of observing emergent systems, without being misguided into thinking that they can be predicted and prescribed. Co-linearity of emergent themes is more likely than sequential impact. Service Thinking firms make multiple experiments at multiple points in time and assess the results dynamically within the emerging service system. They adjust and change flexibly and do not get locked in early to irreversible or rigid strategies. They employ component business models to modularize their structures so that they can add and subtract competencies, internalizing some specializations and externalizing others. They carefully monitor customer behavior and sentiment, and can react quickly when patterns change. They measure the profitability that results from their R-T-I governance models and are guided by the light of outcomes.

With Our Thomas the Tank Engine speculation, we simply hope to illustrate how to start to apply the seven concepts of Service Thinking to support ideas for possibilities in the co-creation and rapid scaling of new value and new profits.

Car-as-a-Service

The evolution of the experience of car ownership and car driving in the 21st century is an illustration of the impact of Service Thinking. In 2013, as this is written, the evolution from product to service in the automobile business is well under way and, in fact, is developing in multiple nonlinear directions.

Let us begin with a widely available offering, the Ford Fusion with Sync. Ford Sync[3] is an early example of a next generation connected software-driven dashboard or vehicle information and communications system. Ford is enhancing its offering via a platform + services strategy. The car and its manufacturing infrastructure is the platform, and software and communications generate the services. This approach opens up pathways to multiple revenue generation streams based on opening up new customer experience options. For example, the "Wi-Fi hotspot" is available in one service package offering but not in others, allowing auto manufacturers to generate revenues from customers that care about such features without having to manufacture a hardware model. Some services in Sync require a subscription, while others are part of a base package. Vehicle health reports, for instance, which send engine diagnostic information to the Ford portal, are available in base packages. Personalized traffic alerts and satellite radio, on the other hand, require a subscription plan. Lastly, features like HD Radio are available as a "pay per song" model, similar to iTunes.

An auto manufacturer, using such a "platform + services" model, could have limitless possibilities for the design of the new customer experiences. Customers can have the option to pay for navigation maps for a short duration, such as a weekend trip, rather than paying a monthly subscription. Manufacturers can also offer entertainment, such as movies or video games, to rent for a weekend or a long trip. Additionally, manufacturers can offer a vehicle's maintenance history in the Cloud. This information will stay with the vehicle and can be passed along to a new owner. An example of this is in General Electric's TRUEngine program which helps GE engine owners "maximize your asset's marketability and ensure it receives the full range of GE's world-class support. Through our online TRUEngine database, appraisers and buyers can quickly confirm an engine's qualification status by Engine Serial Number (ESN)."

Ford has also partnered with an auto insurance provider to track and transmit mileage data, resulting in improved insurance rates for drivers. These creative services provide Ford with experience design opportunities for recurring revenues, in addition to an increase in customer loyalty for not only Ford, but for their entire network, such as their insurance provider partner.

A separate direction for the evolution of car-as-a-service is provided by Zipcar[4] and similar companies such as Car2Go in Europe. Zipcar provides cars parked around cities in pods, available on demand to users for a subscription fee. It's an example an evolutionary service known as shared consumption—using the web and mobile technology to share what used to be products but are now a component of a service platform. The network has become a platform for sharing physical objects, as much as it is a platform for software as a service and Cloud computing.

Zipcar's car sharing service is still an early market to be sure. Many of the users are in cities and are college students. But according to Frost & Sullivan, the revenue from car sharing programs in North America will increase to $3.3 billion in 2016, up from $253 million in 2009.

Despite the small(ish) size of the car sharing market, the next generation of car sharing startups have already emerged in recent months focused on building car sharing around personal vehicles (owned by people in your community or neighborhood instead of an entity like Zipcar). Think of these new businesses as Zipcar without the large capital overhead.

Cars-as-a-service cuts down on the total number of vehicles on the road and uses individual cars much more efficiently. The Internet—through it's social network capabilities—is uniquely able to break up the ownership of a good into an efficiently managed service revolving around access. Service efficiently generates more use out of a single good because service values units of experience over units sold.

These two pathways to car-as-a-service will intersect in Google Driverless Cars. These cars integrate a new component into the service system for automobile usage: the service of operating the vehicle for you. Benefits of service will include comfort, safety, and freeing the driver to be more productive during the journey. It is easy to imagine Google Driverless Cars cruising the city, ready to be called up (via a touchscreen interface on a smartphone) to pick up a passenger at any location and take him to any location, with perhaps some auction bidding software for ride sharing.

The overall service system will be enhanced with better highway speeds (more efficiency) and fewer accidents (new value creation) and more integration between highway safety systems and in-car safety systems. All service system elements will require revision including insurance, traffic authority rules, automobile ownership patterns, and many more.

Google Driverless Cars are mobile by definition and can operate anywhere in the world with a sufficient data and technology platform. The technology is social in exchanging information with drivers, other vehicles, and highway, and safety systems, creating the capacity increase and safety enhancements.

These examples indicate that once we start to apply Service Thinking the opportunities for service Innovation appear endless and exciting.

CHAPTER 9

The Individualization of Opportunity and Your Career

Make a job or take a job!
—James C. Spohrer

Since the 19th century, industrialization has been the enemy of individualization. Scale was the great arbiter of efficiency and it required uniformity. Scale required firms to make large quantities of the same goods, and it often required lots of people doing the same job, repetitively. Companies measured their success based on their size, and on their market share in uniformly defined categories of commodity products.

As business progressed toward the latter half of the 20th century, we became less dependent on scale manufacturing, and a greater percentage of GDP in all economies was generated by services. But many of us were still in thrall to the idea that size is an arbiter of performance for enterprises. We continued to refer to the Fortune 500 and Forbes 2000 lists of the biggest companies as yardsticks of economic and business success. If you wanted to work for a large multinational company, you had to fit their standard requirements, and had to follow their approved educational path (many multinational companies will only recruit from a limited list of top-ranked universities, which eliminates opportunities for equivalent degree holders who do not graduate from those schools). Once inside, you worked on projects of their choosing, and your economic and psychic rewards were determined by climbing their hierarchy.

If you were to choose the entrepreneur route, you were still governed by the economics of scale. If you started a small business, your access to capital and to services such as banking, marketing, legal, and insurance was restricted, as was your access to healthcare. Large-scale outlet owners often blocked distribution, because they demanded high tolls for access. If you sought venture capital, you found that few actually get funding, and it was harder to obtain at the end of the 20th century than in earlier decades.

Service Thinking is transformative, because it counters these restrictions on discovering innovative opportunities. It opens up opportunity to every individual, whether as a business owner, or as a contractor to an industry or a large enterprise, or as a newly liberated employee in a company—or transitioning out of one—who is on the front-line, delivering service to customers. The Service Thinking framework provides unprecedented individualization of opportunity. Let's review to see how.

Service as Experience

As we have emphasized throughout, the evaluation of service quality is subjective and idiosyncratic. This attribute necessarily opens up the path to personalization of service. We probably still have a long way to go before big companies master the concept of personalization of their offerings. But the individual member of the sales staff working with a customer on a software deal, the individual consultant working on a strategy project, the individual manning the front desk for a global hotel chain, the individual plumber called to fix a malfunction, all of these individual roles have the opportunity to deliver to the customer a better experience than would have been the case without them. The new creativity is being close to the customer with the opportunity to provide a service. The opportunities for value creation are unlimited, and the chance to find fulfillment in delivering service is unrestricted.

And, for the individual who prefers to go his or her own way and to be a service entrepreneur, the field is wide open because personalization of service-as-experience for the customer means that there is always the opportunity for service innovation. There can never be an end to it, and there are no effective barriers to entry. The fastest growing type of business in Silicon Valley now is the SEO—Single Employee Operation.[1]

Co-Creation of Value

On the path to personalization, the customer requires a partner. The new definition of customer satisfaction includes the responsiveness of the provider. In some cases, that responsiveness can be digitally provided in its entirety; Amazon.com is the best example of this phenomenon, consistently receiving high marks for service and satisfaction, even though an Amazon.com customer never speaks to a service provider. However, many service businesses will provide co-creation on the front-line through their empowered employees. This is a role in which the individual, from dealmaker to casino dealer, is empowered to co-design, co-evolve, and co-elevate the service experience.

Service Systems

We defined one of the characteristics of service systems as continuous specialization and integration of new services, those that fit in and contribute new value. The individual who is close to the customer, and who commits to humbly seeking an understanding of the needs of the customer, has the potential to become invaluable, to both the customer and the provider he or she represents. The skills of listening and learning, empathetically processing information through the lens of the customer experience, will be the most prized in the Service Thinking enterprise.

Modular Business Architecture

The componentization of business architectures, which will accelerate as enterprises respond to specialization and integration in service systems, places emphasis on the resources that can be deployed to deliver specialized services effectively. It is a resource-based model for business effectiveness, rather than a process model or an IT model. In many of these service components, specialized skills and knowledge will be one of the most prized resources. As components specialize more and more, specialized skills and knowledge become more and more valuable. An individual can devote himself or herself to being the very best resource for a specific skill or knowledge that is required. The skill or knowledge may be applied directly with the customer, through the medium of collaborative software, or possibly via code that the individual designs or writes. In any of these cases or more, the value of the individual who identifies and seizes an opportunity to be the best specialist can only increase.

Glo-Mo-So Scalable Platforms

The great liberation of the scalable plug-in platform is to eliminate the barriers to entry at the door of the distribution system. The individual app developer, the individual blogger and publisher, the individual business research specialist, the individual consultant, the individual wine maker or wine seller, all can gain access to wide, even global, distribution. The individual and small business can leverage global scale components such as FedEx's global distribution and tracking services, Google's web analytics, and Amazon's Cloud Computing. Scale is no longer a barrier. Global-scale-as-a-service is now available to all.

R-T-I and Continuous Learning

A key to service success is continuous learning about customer needs and preferences. Agile companies will run lots of small experiments to identify and refine the offering that resonates, in the confidence that their R-T-I investment allocation system is nimble in its ability to shift resources to support emerging successes. In enterprises with such a governance system, there is unlimited room for the individual with an equally nimble mind, creative in designing service innovations and testing them at low or no cost, and calling on resources only when there is a proven business case. The opportunity for individuals such as this is no longer limited. They are no longer banned to the rubber rooms of special assignment and test marketing; they are now on the leading edge of costless and frictionless experimentation and innovation, the new scientists of specialization and integration. It's an exciting and rewarding place to be.

Multisided Metrics

What will be the new definition of customer satisfaction in the dynamic and ever-changing environment of Service Thinking? What new insights about customer needs will the new data streams and the new analytics uncover? What new questions are waiting to be asked? In these days of big data and analytics, the role of the data scientist becomes highly elevated and even more highly valued. Are you fascinated by natural language analysis of footnotes in annual and quarterly financial reports that can reveal sentiment in the management of public companies that leads to a new investment innovation? Do you love to create visual data displays that become the new dashboards for real time service adjustments? Can you create new analytics to help sports teams identify the value and the consonance of athletes they might want to draft or trade for? The data streams are vast and ever-growing. The access to computing power is unrestricted. It is the creativity of the analyst that is the critical ingredient for metrics and analytics innovation. If this is your field, the world is at your feet.

Your Career: A Better Way to Approach Opportunity

Career development, skills acquisition, and the very nature of work itself change with a Service Thinking mindset. Just as Service Thinking organizations need to learn to orchestrate the swirling change of ever-evolving service systems and the organizational plug-and-play of componentized business models, so individuals may apply the same dynamically adaptive Service Thinking to career planning.

Service innovation and service creativity—bounded by smarter service structures and analytics—will enable more flexible work structures and career paths. Successful entrepreneurs and enterprises will apply Service Thinking to enable more people to achieve better work experiences that they themselves define. Tools and processes enable freedom rather than prescribe the solutions. Thus, *make a job or take a job* is the Service Thinking mantra to navigate your career through the inevitable workplace evolution.

T-Shaped Professionals

Scale-obsessed enterprises imposed unreasonable requirements on their employees. They populated a military-inspired hierarchical organizational architecture with specialists operating in functional silos. If you were a lawyer, a chemist, or an accountant, that specialist designation became your career-long label. If your specialty went out of favor in the enterprise, you had very little option for career adjustment.

Through Service Thinking, you have much more opportunity to avoid the restrictions of specialization and much more opportunity to make contributions that are both broader and deeper. To do so, you need to actively cultivate your T-shapedness, which is the way forward to become more successful.[2]

T-Shaped professionals deliver the benefits of deep problem-solving skills in one area, based on their specific knowledge and expertise, combined with broad complex-communication and collaborative skills across many areas. As knowledge grows exponentially and technology increasingly augments human capabilities, you can better navigate your career by continuously developing your T-Shape experiences and skills. The figure below illustrates this.

T-shapedness also refers to systems thinking or design thinking. T-shaped people are experts in specific technical areas, but also intimately acquainted with the potential systemic impact of their particular tasks or projects. Universities traditionally educate professionals who become specialized in one specific field; we can describe them as I-shaped.[3] But a change in technology or market conditions can quickly devalue the

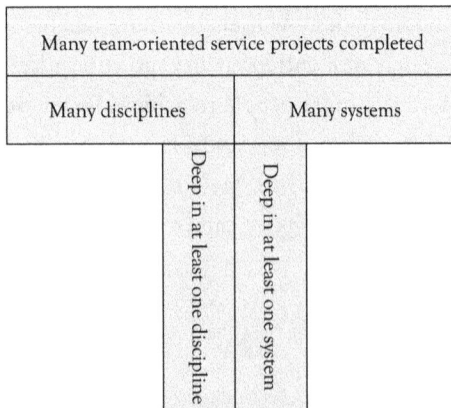

Figure 9.1. T Shape professionals: combining problem solving (deep) and communication (broad) skills.

knowledge and skills of I-shaped professionals. Tim Brown, CEO of IDEO design firm, searched for T-Shaped People for his company. "They have a principal skill that describes the vertical leg of the T—they're mechanical engineers or industrial designers. But they are so empathetic that they can branch out into other skills, such as anthropology, and do them as well. They are able to explore insights from many different perspectives and recognize patterns of behavior that point to a universal human need."[4,5]

Perhaps the most important element of T-shapedness is empathy. Service Thinking values empathy, where understanding the emotional and subjective evaluation of the service experience is critical, and where collaboration in Service Systems and in Co-Creation requires fitting in and humility. If you can examine and understand experiences from another's point of view, without personal or institutional bias, you can become a better Service Thinker.

As a professional in charge of your own career—whether as an employee of a large enterprise, or an entrepreneur – you can manage your own T-shapedness. Dr. Louis Freund, PhD, of the San Jose State University Human Factors and Ergonomics program has developed an assessment technique you can use to measure and augment your T-shapedness. He identifies five areas of "Boundary Crossing Competency" for the T-Top (the horizontal)—such as Professional Development of Self and Others, Education of Self and Others, and variables such as "Improvement" and "knowledge of systems". You can even measure "Likes For Your Blog" and number of Twitter followers (an online personal brand is a very important component of T-shapedness). Similarly, he suggests a number of measures for your T-Stem that cover growth and achievements in your core discipline, whether it is marketing, or engineering or HR. The point is that T-shapedeness can be cultivated and enhanced for a lifetime.

Toward a New Ethos of Service

Rajat Paharia is the founder of Bunchball, a company that exemplifies Service Thinking by building a new business model based on data and gamification to increase customer and employee engagement. (See the profile in Chapter 8.) He suggests that we develop a deep understanding of the primary motivations that make employees and customers happy. He identifies them as:

- **Autonomy**—the urge to direct our own lives ("I Control").
- **Mastery**—the desire to get better at something that matters ("I Improve");
- **Purpose**—the yearning to do what we do in the service of something larger than ourselves ("I Make a Difference").
- **Progress**—the desire to see results in the direction of mastery and the greater purpose ("I Achieve").
- **Social Interaction**—the need to belong, and to be connected to and collaborate with others ("I Connect with Others").[6]

You should identify the goal that motivates you as you navigate your way through your career. If you can use and fulfill these truths about your own innermost desire, you can achieve more engagement and fulfillment through your work. Service Thinking can be a compass to help guide you through what may otherwise be a chaotic and rudderless career journey.

Brand Yourself Through Consonance and Resonance

Do you want lifetime security in a full-time job with the same organization doing the same work in the same way for the rest of your life? Most of these jobs have become commoditized, outsourced, and ultimately automated. Those that have not will disappear soon. The automation of service skills resulting from R-T-I investments in transformation and Glo-Mo-So platforms for scaled digital delivery can affect jobs in many service professions. In Race Against The Machine, Erik Brynjolfsson and Andrew McAfee describe how computer automation of the discovery process in legal cases can enable one lawyer to do the work of 500, and achieve greater accuracy (from 60% accuracy with humans to virtually 100% accuracy with computers).[7] If the legal profession is to be computerized and automated, how long before digital marketing campaigns are automated, eliminating the jobs of professional marketers; how long before healthcare diagnostics and prescriptions of computers are superior to

	Human system	Tool system
Help me by doing some of it for me	Collaborate (incentives) ①	Augment (tool) ②
Help me by doing all of it for me	Delegate (outsource) ③	Automate (self-service) ④
	Organize people (socio-economic models with intentional agents)	Harness nature (Techno-scientific models with stochastic parts)

Z

Example: Call centers

| Collaborate (1970) | → | Augment (1980) | → | Delegate (2000) | → | Automate (2010) |

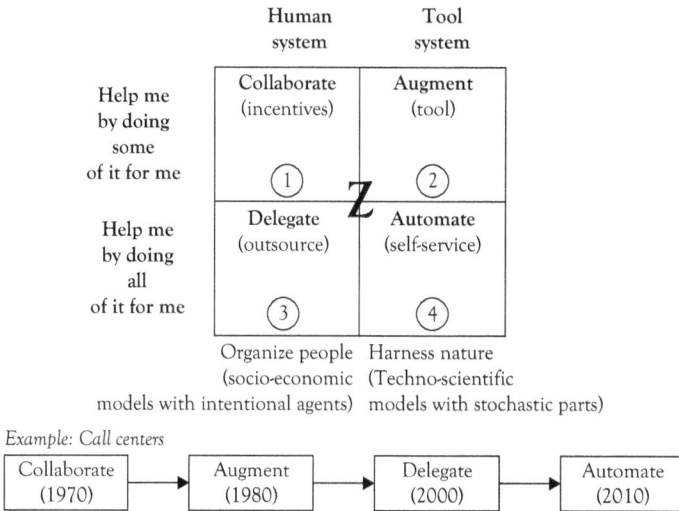

Figure 9.2. *Z Shaped evolution.*

those of doctors. If strategy is emergent, then how long before the number of professional jobs declines in the strategy consulting profession?

Every field of human endeavor will follow what Jim Spohrer and Paul P. Maglio[8] call the Z-shaped evolution of work, in "The emergence of Service Science: Toward systematic service innovations to accelerate co-creation of value."

In the Z-shaped theory, there is a system-encouraged drive in services toward, first, augment ("do some of it for me") and, eventually, automate ("do all of it for me"). Automation occurs when the best practice has been established and can be replicated by computers and software for all customers to experience. In the near future, computational computing will be able to make the decisions for us. Consider Google's driverless car determining its own route based on real time information of traffic patterns. This is just the beginning.

But computers don't have ideas. They have a difficult time cross-fertilizing from one domain of programmed activity to another. They can't sense the emotional needs of human customers as well as another human, nor design the solution to meet those needs. Humans in collaboration with other humans, humans designing and delivering services to other humans, humans with creative ideas for innovative value creation, humans coming up with new combinatorial ideas for the application of existing components in new ways—these will continue to be fields in which fulfilling careers can be built and managed.

How can you manage your career in a world where Service Thinking, componentization, Glo-Mo-So platforms and R-T-I investments in innovation fuel an ever-accelerating drive to technology delivered services? We believe there are five principles:

1. Cast yourself as a contract worker on team projects. Many product manufacturers are switching to service-centricity via outcomes-based contracts. An example is the aircraft engine industry. Many delivery contracts are for "power-by-the hour"—the number of hours of use the engine delivers without the need for maintenance or repair. As a member of a team in this context, you are not , contracting to do the work, but to deliver a certain outcome, so that the experience of your team members and the enterprise is better than it would be without you on the team. Implicitly, you will become good at realizing autonomy (you can move from project to project through different organizations and roles), a specialization (mastery), working with others (collaborative/sharing), and toward a higher purpose (your work will mean something to you).

2. Manage your knowledge and skills development to become a T-shaped individual. The vertical of the T is your depth of specialized knowledge in the field you have chosen. Specialized knowledge, ever evolving, and augmenting, is your primary source of value to others. It makes you a unique contributor. The horizontal on the T is the breadth of knowledge in multiple fields that enables you to integrate your specialized knowledge in the application your team members are developing. It ensures that you fit in and that your specialization is not detached from team goals and methods. T-shaped individuals will be the most valuable practitioners of Service Thinking.

3. Brand yourself through your reputation on previous, present, and future projects, with a network of professional peers who know you and want to work with you. Engage and collaborate and share via blogs, social networks, and posted videos. Build your personal value web. Professional engagement on a Glo/Mo/So platform replaces the standard resume for your improved marketability.

4. Embrace the new creativity. Innovation in service stems from a deep understanding of customers and their needs. Closeness to the customer has become the new locus of creativity. But closeness itself is not enough. Innovative ways to collect and analyze data about customer behavior ("what do they do") are required to yield the understanding of sentiment and motivation (why do they do it? what are they seeking? what is their ultimate goal?) Empathy is required to fully bridge the understanding gap between emotional needs and well-perceived solutions. Sales and everything close to the customer is a rich field of co-creation. Using data and technology in the spirit of Service Thinking will unleash opportunity.

5. Find fulfillment in service. The purpose of service is to make the recipient's life better. Depending on your ambition, this proposition can be elevated to proportions that are global (Smarter Planet), local (Smarter Cities), industry-based (improving healthcare), enterprise-based (transforming your product-centric employer into a service-centric employer), or individual (entrepreneurship). At all these levels, service is a fulfilling and meaningful life's purpose.

In Which Role Should You Base Your Career?

We believe there are four domains to consider (you may find yourself in one or several of these domains during different times in your career).

Entrepreneur

Dr. Pejham and his colleagues developed AsthmaMD to improve the lives of asthma sufferers, using an established Glo-Mo-So platform to enable and scale data collection. The data became useful for physicians in diagnosis and treatment prescription and to researchers to analyze for new breakthroughs in managing the condition. Dr Pejham improved the lives of patients, doctors, and researchers, and also established a business model for himself, his team, and his university.

Entrepreneurship has fewer barriers than ever before. Technology, scalable platforms, fundraising, collaboration, and global distribution—all these are available to entrepreneurs at low or no cost. You need empathy to understand experience gaps, and the ideas to bridge them.

Enterprise Innovation

Do IBM's service transformation or Amazon's use of componentization in the pursuit of service innovation, or FedEx's invention of new service technologies to make the world smaller through faster and more accurate package delivery, inspire you? There are plenty of opportunities to be a team player in the service transformation of global enterprises; there are many product-centric companies that need to transform into service companies to survive and thrive. Your T-shaped skills in bringing Service Thinking into these enterprises can be both productive and fulfilling.

Small- and Medium-Sized Private or Family Business

Job creation occurs disproportionately in small business rather than large ones, as large businesses are automating while small businesses are creating and innovating. A family business can componentize via modular business architecture and scale via Glo-Mo-So platforms just as quickly and effectively as a well-known large enterprise. Manufacturing, assembly, retail, and distribution—small and medium businesses in all these fields can compete on efficiency and win on service. Family wineries are reaching new customers via the web, building communities of loyal users, and selling to the global hotel community. Repair contractors, plumbers, and electricians are using platforms like Angie's List to extend their reach. Apparel designers can make their value proposition directly to targeted customers and build a value constellation of fabric makers, cutters, assemblers, and shippers to deliver customized products at speed. The family business is now a rich field of service innovation and an environment for a fulfilling career.

Vendor to an Industry

Are you inspired to improve healthcare? Do you have an idea for making the legal process more accessible and available to more people? Do you pine to make retail banking more user-friendly? You don't have to work for the insurer or the law firm or the bank. You can join (or create) a vendor who seeks to make that improvement as a service to the industry—perhaps as a specialized business component to be integrated, or as a piece of software to be accessed through the Cloud. Transformational change often comes from the outside of the industry-leading enterprises rather than from the inside (because of the "pull of the past"). You can be on the vendor team that achieves this change.

In any of these fields, the framework concepts of Service Thinking can lead you to "eye opening" insight and problem/opportunity identification in the assessment phase and to the design of new, effective solutions in the response phase. As a T-shaped contributor, you can orchestrate people, knowledge, and technology in new ways to reach new goals, achieve new value, and improve lives.

Summary

If you find benefit using the Service Thinking framework, then we have achieved our purpose. We did not intend to write another business "recipe book" with prescriptive jargon about how, if you follow these steps, you will be successful. We are all navigating our way through times of uncertainty with rapid change. You may have hopes and dreams that you fear will be thwarted by uncontrollable and unanticipated circumstances. Yet, if you can align your aspirations to reality and take ownership of your career and experience in collaboration and in service with others, you can chart a course that will lead to a more purposeful, meaningful and successful career, wherever it will take you.

Afterword

Professional and technical literature is already full of books, for all levels of readers and interests. In fact, I think there are more books out there that we need to know about, let alone read. *Service Thinking* is definitely not "yet another business book." I have found the content inspirational in several unique ways. First, it presents a practical collection of techniques that people will definitely use in actual field-based work. Second, the content invites the reader to have a deep-dive, not an anecdotic description of consulting experiences put together with the intention of creating more branding for the authors. Third, the content is a serious elaboration of a number of services systems ideas without the reader needing to be a business researcher.

The framework that the book introduces covers several dimensions that are among the most commonly encountered when understanding and acting on change in organizations. The target of the framework is services organizations—but understood in a modern sense, where the new economy will show traditionally inward-looking enterprise "service centers" an opportunity to add value beyond the firm, deconstructing traditional value-chains and redefining competition in and across conventional industry boundaries.

I had read another book by the same authors in 2008 (*Improve Your Marketing to Grow Your Business*, Wharton School Publishing) that made visible then the most common trends in enterprise marketing that we see emerging today. This book is another seminal milestone in creating a new generation of more competent business and engineering professionals by providing them interdisciplinary material that comes from many market-proven experiences. This book is then very far from "personal illumination," so typical of those we see from "gurus," done with the pretense of making an isolated experience a new trend for organizations to embrace and voiced by the marketing power of the publishing house. The "new" thing in this book is around a methodology that should be definitely imitated by other business writers, i.e., ingenious and creative approaches based on the evidence of what works in practice (and not only in the practice of one or two people but thousands).

I truly believe this book will be a companion reference for serious consultants either with a business or engineering background. And it will also be used by business and enterprise engineering researchers to revisit and shed new light on those theories that we have been using to approach the modeling and transformation of enterprises. I think each chapter of the book is an invitation to conduct further investigation and to be used in the corresponding class of a graduate curriculum or professional education course. I bet the next edition will double the size of the present one and will show the further evolution of the framework as consumed and improved by practitioners and researchers in the few upcoming years.

Dr. Jorge Sanz
Director Business Analytics Center—National University of Singapore
Chief Innovation Officer Retail Banking—IBM Corporation

Endorsements

In Praise of Service Thinking

Hastings and Saperstein's *Service Thinking* will help everyone become part of the next generation workforce. Their principles impact productivity, quality, compliance, sustainability, resilience, competitive parity, innovativeness, and how to increase them year after year. *Service Thinking* is an excellent primer for all ISSIP (International Society of Service Innovation Professionals) members who aspire to become better T-shaped innovators for business and societal systems with depth and breadth across all interconnected disciplines, sectors, and regions with a Service-Dominant Logic worldview. *Service Thinking* is the introduction of service science for practical business thinkers.

Dr. James C. Spohrer
Director, IBM University Programs Worldwide
Innovation Champion

This is a must-read for anyone trained in traditional process improvement or business architecture. In surprisingly clear language this book lays out the essentials of service thinking, and how the service paradigm transforms the way in which organizations innovate on behalf of their customers. It shifts the focus from product to experience, from one-sided production to co-creation of value, from the simply measurable to the emotional. I intend to buy a copy for every member of my team.

Dart Lindsley,
Sr. Manager of Transformation Planning and Analysis, Cisco

Service thinking is the missing link between a product or service and the consumer. The authors show clearly that it's not enough anymore to just offer the best product or the best service. What's needed is empathy with the customer and understanding of the importance of the overall service experience. A service experience is co-created with the customer. With the 7 Point Service Thinking Framework the authors give any practitioner an invaluable toolset to create a service experience beyond a pure service.

Mario Herger, Senior Innovation Strategist, SAP

Finally, a book that illuminates the massively important service innovation within a total brand experience. This book provides a comprehensive roadmap for electrifying customers. Service is the new "bright shiny object."

Michael Perman
Dean of Global Innovation
Gap, Inc

We all know the world is changing. The challenge is finding a coherent paradigm to make sense of the change and bring clarity to what to do. Service Thinking is a compelling paradigm to help organizations evolve their thinking, processes and structures to meet today's challenges. It's profound yet obvious at the same time. Every business today is a service; Service Thinking provides the framework to adapt to this reality and win.

Doug Milliken, VP, Brand Development, The Clorox Company

This is a must read for anyone who hopes to stay ahead of the curve in the business transformation that is underway. Service Thinking not only reveals why the old business centric models no longer work, but suggests compelling ways that technology, innovation and service can be combined to create value in this new world

Jonathan Levy, Director of Employee Training, Autodesk, Inc.

What makes it a better company than your average taxi or limo company? It provides better service, mostly through much better data (you can see where your ride actually is, for instance). How can your company do the same? Hastings and Saperstein's Service Thinking leads the way in how you can change your organization to provide the innovation that leads to breakthroughs like what Uber is delivering.

Robert Scoble
Startup Liaison Officer
Rackspace—the Open Cloud Company

The role and importance of services in the economy has long been under-appreciated, and poorly understood, by most economists and management consultants. So it is great to see Hastings and Saperstein provide lots of innovative insights around service thinking in this book. Their excellent analysis should be required reading by entrepreneurs and analysts needing to understand the dynamics of our global service economy.

Eilif Trondsen, PhD; Research Director,
Strategic Business Insights (SRI)

Service Thinking is an extraordinary gift to those business leaders committed to taking their organizational game to the next level. Their lenses and language make the Service Thinking paradigm highly accessible. Their prescription of continuous design and redesign of complex business systems is spot on.

Bill Veltrop, Co-Founder *Monterey Institute for Social Architecture*

Preparing graduates to be T-shaped business-ready is a priority at Clarkson. This book is a major achievement to move business education ahead. Every business school should encourage faculty and students to use this as a resource to bridge the chasm between what is taught and needed to prepare students to participate in the emergent economy.

Dayle M. Smith, PhD
Dean, School of Business
Clarkson University

Notes

Introduction

1. Brynjolfsson and McAfee (October 2012).
2. CIA World Factbook (2012).
3. Maglio and Spohrer (2008).
4. Morgan (March 2009).
5. Normann and Ramirez (July/August 1993).
6. Von Mises (March 2007).
7. Mitra (June 2013).

Chapter 1

1. Ibid.
2. IBM.Com/SmarterPlanet.
3. Irene Ng (2012).
4. Harmon (July 2008).
5. Sanz (2013).
6. Paharia (June 2013).
7. Schultz, Howard and Gordon, Joanne (2011).
8. Investor.Starbucks.com.

Chapter 2

1. Smith (1776).
2. Von Mises (1949).
3. Bitner (March 2007).
4. http://ibmsmartcamp.com/2013/09/28/ibm-smartcamp-silicon-valley-perspective-from-hult-professor-jeff-saperstein-cloud-and-analytics-will-transform-everything/
5. Hastings and Saperstein (October 2007).
6. Chesbrough (December 2006)
7. Wall Street Journal (February 2013).

Chapter 3

1. Atlantic Monthly (February 2013).
2. Peter Drucker (1954).
3. Kissmetrics Blog (2013).

Chapter 4

1. Levinson (October 2002).
2. Sanford & Taylor (2005)

Chapter 5

1. Nilofer Merchant (September 2012).
2. Pohle, Korsten, Ramamurthy, Froecking (2005).
3. Williams (January 2013)
4. Saylor (June 2012)
5. Eggers, Jason Salzetti (February 2013), Governing.com
6. Courley (2012).
7. National Hospital Ambulatory Medical Care Survey (2009).
8. SteveandKatesCamp.com.

Chapter 6

1. Geoffrey Moore (2011).
2. John Arthur Ricketts (2008).
3. Robert Litan (2010).
4. Information Week (April 2009).
5. UKEssays.com.
6. Johanna Cox (October 2012).
7. Shelly Banjo (Feb, 2013).
8. Richart McGill Murphy (2006).
9. Craig Newmark (March 2013).

Chapter 7

1. Von Mises (2008).
2. Marchand and Peppard (January 2013-February 2013).
3. Davenport (February 2013).
4. Glissmann, Sanz, Liu, Becker (2012).

5. Anderson, Kumar, Narus (2004).
6. Zeithaml, Jo Bitner, Gremler (2009).
7. Reicheld (2006).
8. The Neilsen Company (April 2012).
9. Forrester Consulting (September 2008).
10. Paharia (2013).
11. www.gallup.com/strategicconsulting/157451/state-american-workplace
    -2008-2010.aspx.
12. Gartner November 28th Gamification Trends and Strategies to Help Prepare for
    the Future. Burke.B. http://www.gartner.com/it/content/2191900/2191918/
    november_28_gamification_bburke.pdf?userID=61080590

Chapter 8

1. Wikipedia (n.d.).
2. Aziz (2012, November).
3. Anant (2013, January)
4. Fehrenbacher (2011, April).

Chapter 9

1. Tam (March 2010).
2. Paharia (May 2013).
3. Brynjolfsson, McAfee (2011).
4. Donofrio, Spohrer, and Zadeh (2010).
5. Iansiti (1993).
6. Brown (2005).
7. Brown (2009).
8. Spohrer and Maglio (2006).

References

Aziz, P. (2012). *3D printed Aston Martin debuts In Bond's 'Skyfall'.* Retrieved on November 13, 2012 from Psfk: http://www.psfk.com/2012/11/3d-printed-aston-martin-skyfall.html

Banjo, S. (2013, February 25). Targeting tech-savvy startups. *Wall Street Journal.*

Bashyam, A. (2013, January 8). Car-as-a-service era is here. *EE Times.*

Boulton, C. (2013, February 4). Peter Diamandis says enterprises must crowdsource to compete. *Wall Street Journal.*

Brown, T. (2005). Strategy By Design, *Fast Company*, June.

Brown, T. (2009). *Change By Design: How Design Thinking Transforms. Organizations and Inspires Innovation.* New York, NY; Harper Business.

Brynjolfsson, E., & McAfee, A. (2011). *Race against the machine.* Digital Frontier Press.

Chesbrough, H. (2006). *Open Innovation.* Boston, MA: Harvard Business School PressChung, Po. (2012). *Service Reborn.* Belvedere, CA: Lexingford Press.

Central Intelligence Agency (2012). *World Factbook.* U.S.A.: Directorate of Intelligence.

Courley, S. (2012). *Big data and the rise of augmented intelligence.* Retrieved December, 2012, from TEDxAuckland: http://tedxtalks.ted.com/video/Big-Data-and-the-Rise-of-Augmen

Davenport, T. (2013, February 13). P&G finds a goldmine in Analytics. *Wall Street Journal.*

Drucker, P. (1954). *The practice of management.* New York, NY: Harper Business.

Donofrio, N., Spohrer, J., & Zadeh, H. S. (2010). *Research driven medical education and practice: A case for T-shaped professionals.* Retrieved on 2010 from http://www.ceri.msu.edu/wp-content/uploads/2010/06/A-Case-for-T-Shaped-Professionals-20090907-Hossein.pd

Eggers, W. & Salzetti, J. (2013). *Mobile technology, co-creation and the empowered citizen.* Retrieved February 13, 2013, from Governing: the states and localities: http://www.governing.com/columns/mgmt-insights/col-co-creation-mobile-technology-government-service-delivery.html

Farr, C. (2012). *Enterprise is sexy! 80% of tech startups likely to IPO are B2B.* Retrieved December 6, 2012, from VentureBeat: http://venturebeat.com/2012/12/06/cb-insight/

Foley, J. (2009). *IBM CIO's strategy: run, transform, innovate.* Retrieved April 30, 2009, from InformationWeek: http://www.informationweek.com/global-cio/interviews/ibm-cios-strategy-run-transform-innovat/229206998

Forrester Consulting (2008). *How engaged are your customers.* Cambridge, MA: Forrester Research.

Glissmann, S., Sanz, S., Liu, R., & Becker, V. (2012). Disentangling the value of information and analytics through componentized business architecture. *45th Hawaii International Conference on System Sciences,* 4250–4259.

Hsu, C. (2012). *Burberry tops the charts again in fashion index.* Retrieved October 5, 2012, from L2 the Daily: http://www.l2thinktank.com/burberry-tops-the-charts-again-in-fashion-index/2012

Harmon, P. (2008, July). Governance and maturity. *Business Process Trends 1(7),* 1–2.

Hastings, H., & Saperstein, J. (2007). *How to improve your marketing to grow your business.* Upper Saddle River, NJ: Pearson-Wharton Business School.

Honigman, B. (2013). *10 ways to make customers fall in love with your business.* Retrieved on May 5, 2013, from Kissmetrics: http://blog.kissmetrics.com/true-love-with-customers/

Iansiti, M. (1993). Real World R&D: Jumping The Product Generation Gap, *Harvard Business Review* May-June.

IBM Smarter Planet. Retrieved from: http://www.ibm.com/smarterplanet/us/en/index.html.

Investor.Starbucks.com.

Jo Bitner, M. (2007). *Keeping promises: Closing the services gap.* Retrieved March 28, 2007, from KnowWPC: http://knowwpcarey.com/article.cfm?aid=658

Kumar, N., Anderson, J. C., & Narus, J. A. (2007). *Value merchants: Demonstrating and documenting superior value in business markets.* Boston, MA: Harvard Business School Press.

Litan, R. (2010). *Inventive billion dollar firms: A faster way to grow?* Kansas City, MO: Kauffman Foundation.

Media and entertainment (2012). *Global trust in advertising and brand messages.* New York, NY: Nielsen.

Marchand, D. & Peppard, J. (2013, January–February). Why IT fumbles analytics. *Harvard Business Review.*

Merchant, N. (2012, September). 11 rules for creating value in the social era. *Harvard Business Review.*

Mitra, S. (2013). *How to reduce "infant entrepreneur mortality".* Retrieved June 10, 2013, from Harvard Business Review: http://blogs.hbr.org/2013/06/how-to-reduce-infant-entrepren/

Moore, G. (2011). *Escape velocity.* New York, NY: HarperBusiness.

Moore, G. A. (2011). *Escape velocity: Free your company's future from the pull of the past.* New York, NY: HarperCollins.

Morgan, A. (2009). *Eating the big fish: How challenger brands can compete against brand leaders (2nd ed.).* Hoboken, NJ: Wiley.

Murphy, R. M. (2006, April). Zero to $1 billion. *CNNMoney.*

National Hospital Ambulatory Medical Care Survey: 2009 Outpatient Department Summary Tables, table 11 [PDF - 330 KB])

Newmark, C. (2013). *Big IT at the Veterans Affairs*. Retrieved on March, 2013, from LinkedIn: http://www.linkedin.com/today/post/article/20130301220621-5062-big-it-development-at-dept-of-vets-affairs

Ng, Irene (2012). *Value & worth: Creating new markets in the digital economy*. InnovorsaPress.

Normann, R., & Ramirez, R. (1993, July/August). From value chain to value constellation: Designing interactive strategy. *Harvard Business Review 71(4)*.

Paharia, R. (2013). *Loyalty 3.0: How big data and gamification are revolutionizing customer and employee engagement* (Kindle Locations 296–302). New York, NY: McGraw Hill.

Pohle, G., Korsten, P., Ramamurthy, S., & Froecking, S. (2005). The specialized enterprise: A fundamental redesign of firms and industries. New York, NY: IBM Institute for Business Value.

Ricketts, J. A. (2008). *See reaching the goal: How managers improve service business using Goldratt's theory of constraints*. Indianapolis, IN: IBM Press.

Reicheld, F. (2006). How NPS Can Drive Growth. In F. Reicheld (Ed.), *The ultimate question*. Boston, MA: Harvard Business School Press.

Sanford, L., & Taylor, D. (2005). *Let go to grow: Escaping the commodity trap*. Upper Saddle River, NJ: Prentice Hall.

Sanz, J. (2013). *IEEE: Enabling customer experience and front-office transformation through business process engineering*. Vienna, Austria: CBI 2013 Conference on Business Informatics.

Saylor, M. (2012). *The mobile wave: How mobile intelligence will change everything*. New York, NY: Vanguard Press.

Scaggs, A. (2013, May). Tepid profits, roaring stocks. *Wall Street Journal*.

Schultz, H., & Gordon, J. (2011). *Onward: How Starbucks fought for its life without losing its soul*. Emmaus, PA: Rodale

Spohrer, J. C., & Engelbart, D. C. (2004). Converging technologies for enhancing human performance: Science and business perspectives. *Annals of the New York Academy of Sciences 1013*(1), 50–82.

Spohrer, J. C.& Maglio, P. M. (2006) Service Science, Management, and Engineering: An Emerging Multidiscipline. IBM Research—Yorktown presentation on Oct. 20, 2006. Slide #80 Speaker notes: Spohrer—Engelbart Cycle of Service System Evolution (Augmentation Systems: Bootstrapping Capability Infrastructure via Coevolution of Human System and Tool System). URL: http://www.slideshare.net/spohrer/spohrer-and-maglio-yorktown-20061020-v2

Spohrer, J. C., & Maglio, P. M. (2010). The emergence of Service Science: Toward systematic service innovations to accelerate co-creation of value. IBM Research Center, Almaden.

Smith, A. (1776). *An Inquiry into the Nature and Causes of the wealth of nations*: London Edition. University of Chicago Press.

Tam, P. (2010, March). When Just One Desk Will Do. *Wall Street Journal.*

Thompson, D. (2013, February). How airline ticket prices fell 50% in 30 years (and why nobody noticed). *Atlantic Monthly.*

Vargo, S. L., & Lusch, R. F. (2004). Evolving to a new dominant logic for marketing. *Journal of Marketing,* (January) 68:1–17.

Von Mises, L. (2010). Human action: The scholar's edition. In Human action: The Scholar's edition (p.178), (location 386 in iBooks). Auburn, AL: Ludwig von Mises Institute.

Wikipedia (n.d.). 3D printing.

Williams, A. (2013). Forrester Research: SaaS and data-driven "smart" apps fueling worldwide software growth. TechCrunch.

Zeithaml, V., Jo Bitner, M., & Gremler, D. (2009). *Services marketing: Integrating customer focus across the firm* (6th ed.). McGraw Hill Irwin.

Index

www.ingramcontent.com/pod-product-compliance
Lightning Source LLC
Chambersburg PA
CBHW050124210326
41519CB00015BA/4094